AMERICAN ISSUES

BOOK 3

A Government of Lies, Corruption, Murder, & Treason

By
Tyson Johnson

I'm Not an Extremist, Right Wing, Left wing, Republican, Democrat, Conservative, Liberal Socialist, Communist, or Insurrectionist; I'm just a Pro-American Earth Born Citizen trying to live the life that I was born to live without being Lied to, Deceived, Abused by, Corrupted by, Controlled by, Extorted by or Enslaved by this or any other Government.

© Tyson Johnson

Paperback ISBN: 979-8-89283-257-1
Ebook ISBN: 979-8-89283-258-8

The 3rd addition of the American Issues Series.
Highlighting the damaging issues and people that are playing a huge roll in the destruction of the United States of America.

Tyson Johnson
15370 Cholame Rd. #6
Victorville, California 92392
www.TysonJohnson.com

Knowledge is Power
If you know and understand what they're doing to you and what they're attempting to do to you, then you'll be better equipped to resist and prevent yourself, your kids, and the future of this country from becoming subservient slaves to a Tyrannical Totalitarian Government.

Liability Waiver

The information contained in this book is based on the author's extensive research, interviews, and reading. While every effort has been made to ensure the accuracy of the information presented, the author makes no guarantees regarding the completeness, reliability, or suitability of the content. There is some information contained in this book series that you may not want to hear and/or some information that you may not want to believe, but in today's world, it's hard to hide the truth. There is a lot to think about and a lot to consider. The Truth Hurts Sometimes!

The reader acknowledges that the information may not be completely accurate or up to date and agrees that any reliance on such information is at their own risk. The author shall not be liable for any claims, losses, emotional turmoil, mental illness, or damages of any type arising from the use or interpretation of the information contained in this book.

Some of the thoughts, ideas, and expressions in this book are personal thoughts and opinions of the author and should not be construed purposely as slanderous or defamatory to any person, business, or entity, whether associated with the Government or Civilian class.

By reading this book, the reader agrees to waive any and all claims against the author, publisher, or any affiliates related to the content provided.

Read, Learn, and Grow at Your Own Risk...

The First Amendment to the Constitution primarily protects the constitutional right to FREE SPEECH in the United States. This amendment states, "Congress shall make no law... abridging the freedom of speech, or of the press." Here's a breakdown of what this right entails:

1. **Freedom of Expression:** *The First Amendment protects not only spoken words but also written communication, symbolic speech (like protests or demonstrations), and other forms of expression, including art and music.*

2. **Right to Voice Opinions:** *Individuals have the right to express their opinions, beliefs, and ideas without government interference. This includes both popular and unpopular viewpoints.*

3. **Limitations:** *While free speech is a fundamental right, it is not absolute. There are certain limitations, such as:*
   - *Speech that incites violence or poses a direct threat to public safety.*
   - *Obscenity or child pornography.*
   - *Defamation or slander that falsely harms someone's reputation.*
   - *Certain types of hate speech may also face restrictions, depending on the context.*

4. **Public vs. Private Spaces:** *The right to free speech primarily protects individuals from government censorship. In private settings, such as workplaces or social media platforms, organizations may impose their own rules regarding speech.*

5. **Importance in Democracy:** *Free speech is essential for a democratic society, allowing for open debate, the exchange of ideas, and the ability to challenge government actions.*

Overall, the First Amendment enshrines the right to express oneself freely, fostering a culture of dialogue and dissent that is vital to a healthy democracy.

Dedication

This book is dedicated to the Americans who were raised believing in an American Dream, a Free Country, and a Better Way of Life, but instead were enslaved by this greedy, tyrannical, and corrupt government.

We were born free and deserve to live without corruption, greed, government overreach, over-taxation, and the lies we've all been told since the day we were born. This Dedication is for those who suffered through the evil doings of our own government against the citizens of this country.

Dedicated to all the Veterans who fought for this country and what it was supposed to stand for, only to end up homeless, hungry, and without proper medical care.

The American citizens who have no home or daily food watching their own government spend American tax dollars building houses and hospitals and feeding foreign families in foreign countries while ignoring our own.

And to the hard-working Americans who sacrifice daily, get up at all hours to commute to a thankless job where they work countless hours. These people are then overtaxed by a greedy, corrupt government who then operate countless money laundering schemes (U.S.A.I.D.) to fill their pockets and the pockets of their corporate and political friends. They extort the citizens through the IRS using force and fear, Taxing working families to the brink of poverty while not improving our country and just giving our money away to lazy free-loading people, illegal aliens, foreign nationals and foreign countries for foreign wars.

Prologue

Call them the "Deep State," the "Elite," "The Shadow Government," "Military Industrial Complex," and you can also call them "Leaders" of the United States who have been in control and destroying the lives of the American people for as long as America has been around. None of these Tyrannical criminals are our leaders; they are merely representatives, and they should be reminded of that fact and put in their place!

Some say that possibly they're the evil descendants of those who controlled the English Colonizers back when they first successfully arrived on this continent (1607). Some say that the Revolutionary War (1775-1783) may have given us direct freedom from British rule, but England kept their "Elite" families (spies/double agents) here undercover to destroy America from within. The possibility that the "Swamp" was created and kept alive by any and all who joined their cult. This possibility is seen in their actions throughout the history of the United States.

This U.S. Government is so corrupted that it needs strong oversight; the problem is that we've let this go on for so long and not stopped them soon enough that they've created laws to protect themselves from us and prosecution, distanced themselves from us and they've weaponized themselves against us using our "so-called law enforcement" to detain and restrain us from getting to and stopping them! We've allowed them to have power they aren't supposed to have and now, they have that feeling of invincibility as they lord over us.

As humans, we were all born of this planet. No Government created us or the earth and should have no dominion over us. Who are they to control us and our lives? We have the right to live and prosper, fish, collect firewood, start and run a business, say what we like or don't, as long as we aren't infringing on anybody else's lives or rights to being a "Free Spirited Body" of this world or committing any of the basic crimes. We shouldn't have to pay to live on Earth.

No one should be responsible/forced to support the Government (by Force or Fear/Extortion), free-loaders, and definitely not any Foreigners/Refugees/Asylum Seekers with their own hard-earned money unless they, of course, want to. The government shouldn't have free access to our lives, children, or money to do what they choose, nor should they be able to make endless laws (that they don't even adhere to) that force control over us and give them more power to control our lives.

In this book, we'll question the mysterious ways of how Government officials on a salary of $160,000+ annually end up as multimillionaires!

Infamy in America

On this day, December 7th, 1941, A horrible tragedy occurred as America was attacked. Each year, we spend 24 hours remembering, reminiscing, and regretting the actions on that day. Our sadness overwhelms us all for those lives that were lost. Soon after, America rose up as a Country with determination to have a future, and we defeated All of our enemies who stood to destroy us and take that future away! With "WAR" we wiped our enemies out, became the #1 World Power, and secured a Freedom and an American way of life that Only Americans could enjoy without Tyranny!

So many years later and now the Attack on America comes from within! Our own Government Officials and Misguided People have and continue to Attack America to Destroy the American way of life and its Future!

Now Americans are Forced to pay outrageous amounts of Taxes, Fees, and Licenses while also being Forced to Pay for Foreigners who have vowed to destroy America, Illegal Aliens who are already criminals just for entering our country and freely receiving aid (food, money, housing, medical care and driver's licenses) that our own citizens have to qualify for, we pay for the lazy, no good unproductive masses that live better than many hard-working Americans trying to feed their own families!

Americans are Now Under Attack by its own Disloyal people and are quickly being divided and destroyed with very little resistance! War has been declared and is being carried out by those who wish to control you, change your American way of life, take your freedoms away, and enslave you while destroying the future of your Country that your Children and Grandchildren will never know.

Years from now, you'll be watching these same shows and maybe you'll see the same historical memories about how the United States used to be and what life was like when we were Free! You'll see how these internal enemies created mass homeless and hungry Americans while feeding and housing illegal immigrants and Foreign Nationals. You'll see American Businesses being put out and shut down because our Dictators commanded that we must shut them down at their command regardless of the bills we have to pay and families we have to feed. Only Corporate businesses that support their narratives will be allowed to operate and support themselves.

America is Under Attack and Dying at the hands of these Tyrants/Dictators. The Axis of Evil is embedded right here in our own Country. Will you watch it happen, go down with the ship, stand by, and see your children's American future disappear, or will you Stand Up, Fight Back, and make sure that We Patriotic Americans once again Win This War?!

This is a Time that will live in INFAMY.......Save America, Save your Life, Save your Future!

#Stand Up - #Fight Back- #Secure Your Future - #Save Your Family - #Save the Future of America - #America First - #Don't Give Up - #Take America Back

By, Tyson Johnson / December 7, 2020

> **I'm an old-school, small government, keep your nose outta my life and hands outta my pocket kinda guy.**

TABLE OF CONTENTS

Chapter 1: The U.S. Government Hates Americans 10

Chapter 2: The CIA and FBI Hate America 14

Chapter 3: Government Officials Are Supposed To Work For Americans 20

Chapter 4: All Government Officials should be Audited Yearly 22

Chapter 5: Personal Responsibility You Pay for Yours and I'll Pay for Mine 27

Chapter 6: Funding Foreign Nations 31

Chapter 7: Systematic Corruption by the U.S. Government 34

Chapter 8: Accountability and Transparency in Government 37

Chapter 9: False Advertising Laws -What happened to Product Integrity 40

Chapter 10: AMERICAN LAWS 45

Chapter 11: America First 48

Chapter 12: The U.S. Constitution 51

Chapter 13: A.C.L.E. AMERICAN CITIZENS LAW ENFORCEMENT 54

Chapter 14: Censorship in America 56

Chapter 15: American Tax Money to Support Illegal Aliens / Refugees / Foreigners
.... 60

Chapter 16: They're Poisoning Our Food 65

Chapter 17: Government Covert Tests on Americans 76

Chapter 18: Growing Up with Lies and False Flag Attacks 82

Chapter 19: Medical Profits / Medicine for.. Money 97

Chapter 20: Exposing the Government Corruption 104

Chapter 21: A World of Superstitions, Cults, Secret Societies and Religions 114

Chapter 22: Taxing Americans into Poverty 119

CHAPTER 1

THE U.S. GOVERNMENT HATES AMERICANS

Our U.S. Government should always put "America First." The lives, infrastructure, and health of this country and its people should always be paramount. If they spend all their time and our money playing "World Police and Micro-Manager" to every other nation, how can they put in the time, money, and effort into tending to their own flock that is diminishing?

A strong foundation will hold up the frame, but a weak one shall fall. A poorly kept house is a bad example for the rest of the world. If you can't take care of your own house, how can you take care of any other?

A theory on the perception that the American government is destroying America and its citizens because it spends most of its time trying to find more ways to control and diminish the rights of its people, rather than strengthening and helping them to prosper, could be framed around several key themes:

1. **Systemic Issues**: Critics argue that the government operates within a framework that prioritizes the interests of a select few over the general populace. This includes lobbying efforts that favor corporations and wealthy individuals, resulting in policies that may undermine public welfare, such as inadequate healthcare, education, and infrastructure.

2. **Economic Factors***: The growing wealth gap is often cited as evidence of governmental failure. The theory posits that economic policies favoring deregulation and tax cuts for the wealthy have led to decreased funding for social programs. This has resulted in increased poverty levels and diminished access to essential services for many citizens.

3. **Social Policies**: The government's approach to issues like healthcare, education, and criminal justice can be seen as detrimental to the well-being of citizens. For example, the high cost of healthcare and student debt can lead to financial ruin for many families, perpetuating cycles of poverty and limiting opportunities for upward mobility.

4. **Power Dynamics**: The theory also examines the role of political power and influence. It suggests that the concentration of power in the hands of a few leads to decision-making that does not reflect the needs or desires of the majority. This

disconnection can foster a sense of disenfranchisement among citizens, leading to the belief that the government is working against their interests.

5. **Crisis Management**: The government's response to crises—whether economic downturns, public health emergencies, or civil unrest—can also be scrutinized. Critics argue that inadequate or mismanaged responses exacerbate existing problems, further alienating citizens and diminishing trust in government institutions.

In summary, this theory suggests that a combination of systemic failures, economic disparities, social injustices, and concentrated power contributes to the perception that the American government is undermining the well-being of its citizens. This perspective calls for critical examination and major reforms to realign government actions with the needs of the people of the United States.

WHAT THE U.S. GOVERNMENT HAS TAUGHT ME AND THE REST OF AMERICA

When you want your Country to fail, you destroy it from within. Demonstrate, Act, and Encourage the worst in people.

1. Lying is okay; there is no profit in truth.
2. Killing / Murder is okay. No Witness = No Proof / No Crime.
3. Greed is okay. More Money = More Power.
4. Tyranny is okay.
5. Theft is okay.
6. Covering up your crimes is okay.
7. Slavery is okay; forcing your citizens to give you money they work for is acceptable.
8. Corruption is okay.
9. Intimidation is okay.
10. Fraud is okay.
11. Aggressive governing is okay.
12. Cheating is okay.
13. Pedophilia is okay.
14. Censorship is okay.
15. Over-Taxation, Charging Excessive Fees and Licenses is okay.
16. Treason is okay.
17. Genocide is okay.
18. Extortion is okay.
19. I don't have to be accountable for my actions.
20. The U.S. Government is Not "For the People, By the People", they are for themselves.
21. Our Government/Congress is a Dictatorship with no moral oversight.
22. Laws are meant to be broken. You can pick and choose which laws you want to follow.
23. The U.S. Constitution can be ignored, changed, and manipulated.
24. I do not have to follow or obey the law if I have a racial or political agenda.
25. Aborting babies is okay, killing American citizens before they're even born is what's best.
26. Forcing people into your beliefs is okay.
27. Infecting your citizens with viruses and deadly vaccines is okay..
28. Forcing / taxing your citizens in to poverty is okay, as long as you're feeding refugees and immigrants.
29. Letting your Country's Veterans live homeless and hungry while giving free food and housing to illegal immigrants and refugees is okay.
30. Looting, assault/battery, and the destruction of property is okay when protesting.
31. We have the worst Anti-American Government officials in American history.
32. We have the worst group of Anti-American Citizens this country has ever had and will fall because of them.
33. Instilling fear in your citizens is okay, they're easier to control that way.
34. Voting doesn't matter because Your votes don't count, Elections are easily rigged.
35. It's okay to decide on your own which laws will be enforced or ignored.
36. Politicians are Above the Law.
37. Politicians can break the law and never get punished.
38. It's okay to set your own cities on fire, burning down your citizens homes and businesses so that you can rebuild "Smart Cities".
39. You can extort and over-tax all your citizens in to poverty, take all their money and then launder it by giving it to foreign aid causes that give you a huge kickback.

Don't Wait - It's Going to be too Late!
The invasion is here / the Civil War has Already begun!

By, Tyson Johnson

Ok American Citizens who love this Country and are ready to Defend it, Do you NOT See it? We're Very Late to the war, so Get your Guns out and start Defending! The war has already started and we're all just sitting here reading and posting crap on Facebook! The enemy has been here and continues to make changes to defeat us.

They currently have the upper had as they -

1. Continue to manipulate people in the News, in Movies, on TV and Social Media.
2. They put their puppet in to office to charm people in to allowing refugees to be imported.
3. They are putting their Foreign / American Hating agents into Government Positions.
4. They're making laws against American Citizens but benefit Foreigners & illegals.
5. They give a Free Living and Tax Free opportunities to illegals and make us pay for it.
6. They are driving up our Cost of Living and driving American families in to Poverty.
7. They want open borders to flood this country with their foreign agents.
8. They are putting the Fear in to Citizens and making them think they have No Choice.
9. They're making themselves Multi-Millionaires and stealing from us with Over-Taxation.
10. They're feeding/housing the Lazy & Foreigners with our Tax money while we starve.
11. They feed/house Foreigners while American Veterans & Families Suffer in the streets.
12. They're brainwashing our youth to hate our Law Enforcement, Military and Constitution.
13. They make laws to protect themselves and their positions of Power over us all.
14. They make it easier for Illegals to get Benefits than Veterans or US Citizens.
15. They are making a future world that will enslave/control your children & grand children.

The Over-Powered Politicians are destroying our Country and our American Citizens at a rapid pace, enough is enough, will we just sit here and watch it happen or Pick Up our Weapons and
START FIGHTING BACK?!
Politicians should NOT have control over our personal lives or labored money, nor should our Government be able to use OUR tax money for ANYTHING other than American prosperity and improvements. They should ONLY be working on a modest working mans salary (that is intensely watched for signs of bribery and tax fraud) for the security and future of **our United States of America!**

*

* I want to thank the United States Government for the lifelong list of lies and deceit they have instilled in me and all the loyal citizens of this once-great Country. Thank you for showing the children that morals, integrity and hard work will get you nowhere! Thank you for betraying the legal, hard-working citizens of this country, along with the memories of all the Veterans who died making this Country great!

Thank you for destroying the American Dream and the American Way of Life. You've shown the world that a Free Democratic Nation and its ideals cannot survive with traditional corrupt and greedy Politicians in power! Thank you for destroying the Future of this country and putting us next in the history books of great Nations that have imploded. Thank you for taxing us into poverty and destroying everything our forefathers worked so hard to build, then turning us over to foreign nations to finish us off. Thank you all for absolutely Nothing!

CHAPTER 2

THE CIA AND FBI HATE AMERICA

The perception that agencies like the CIA and FBI have turned against and have been weaponized against America and its citizens can stem from various factors, including political polarization, public mistrust, and specific incidents that have led to scrutiny of these organizations.

1. **Political Polarization**: In recent years, the U.S. has experienced heightened political divisions and treasonous activities. Seemingly Corrupt Actions taken by intelligence agencies can be interpreted differently depending on political beliefs, leading some to view them as partisan or untrustworthy.

2. **High-Profile Controversies**: Events such as the investigation into Russian interference in the 2016 elections, surveillance practices revealed by whistleblowers, and the handling of various unwarranted criminal investigations against a former President and citizens who may go against the narrative have raised concerns about overreach and lack of accountability.

3. **Transparency Issues**: Both agencies operate with a level of secrecy that is essential for national security but can also breed suspicion. When information is withheld from the public, it can lead to speculation about their motives and actions.

4. **Civil Liberties Concerns**: Certain policies and practices, especially in counterterrorism and surveillance, have raised alarms about the potential infringement on civil liberties and privacy rights of citizens. They were created to better our country

5. **Media Representation**: Coverage of these agencies can sometimes emphasize negative aspects, contributing to a narrative that they are acting against the interests of the public.

These factors combined can create a narrative that suggests a disconnect between these agencies and the citizens they are meant to serve. It's important to approach these topics with a critical eye and consider multiple perspectives to gain a more comprehensive understanding.

Even now, in February of 2025, the new Presidential administration and Attorney General of the United States is attempting to "Declassify" important U.S. History secrets that have hidden lies from the American people for many decades. Secrets such as the assassination of JFK, his brother Bobby Kennedy, Martin Luther King Jr., 9/11 and the Jeffery Epstein Island list of names. However, something that should be simple to produce, just isn't getting to the AG's desk as requested. All the unredacted documents are being withheld by the upper administration of the FBI, they clearly have a lot to hide from the American people when the AG has to threaten upper FBI administration personnel with indictments just to get the documents.

Their illegal covert operations have been carried out "AGAINST" the American people and there are obviously very powerful guilty parties that are still alive and being protected from exposure and prosecution!

The assertion that the Department of Justice (DOJ) has been "weaponized" against the American people and former/current President Donald Trump is a perspective often expressed in political discourse, particularly by Trump's supporters, and there is now a lot of evidence to prove it. We can only hope that they are all fired, prosecuted, and put in prison where they belong. 9 FBI Agents who participated in the raid on Donald Trump's estate have already filed a lawsuit to stop their identities from being exposed. So many guilty parties...

1. **Investigations and Prosecutions:** Citizens argue that investigations, such as the Mueller investigation into Russian interference in the 2016 election, were politically motivated and aimed at undermining Trump's presidency. Some believe that the DOJ's actions during this period were influenced by political agendas, and has since been proven.

2. **FBI Raids and Searches:** The FBI's execution of search warrants on Trump's properties, including Mar-a-Lago, is often highlighted as an example of the DOJ being used as a tool against a political opponent. Supporters of Trump view these actions as excessive and politically driven by his political opponents, Obama, Clinton, and Biden.

3. **Selective Enforcement:** The DOJ has applied laws and regulations unevenly, favoring certain political groups or individuals (The Democratic Left) while targeting others, particularly those aligned with Trump or conservative movements.

4. **Public Communication:** Many statements made and actions by DOJ officials or the FBI regarding investigations have created a narrative that is damaging to Trump and his supporters, leading to perceptions of bias within these institutions.

5. **Political Appointments:** The strategic appointment of individuals to key positions within the DOJ who have expressed Far-Left political views or taken actions perceived as partisan is often cited as evidence of the department being influenced by political motivations.

Public trust or distrust in governmental institutions like the Department of Justice (DOJ) is influenced by a variety of factors, such as these:

1. **Transparency:** How open and transparent an institution is about its processes, decisions, and actions can significantly impact public perception. Lack of transparency, as we've had for as far back as we can remember, can lead to suspicion and distrust.

2. **Accountability:** Institutions that demonstrate accountability for their actions, including addressing misconduct or errors, tend to foster greater trust. Conversely, a perceived lack of accountability can erode confidence. Unfortunately, the U.S. DOJ believes that they are above the law and take no responsibility or accountability for all the illegal activities that they commit.

3. **Political Influence:** Perceptions of political bias or undue influence in decision-making can lead to distrust. If the public believes that an institution is being used for political gain and weaponized by the Deep State, then confidence can be and has been diminished.

4. **Media Coverage:** The way media is led to report on governmental actions can shape public perceptions. Sensationalized or biased reporting can contribute to distrust, while balanced coverage can enhance understanding and trust. Unfortunately, the media is told when and how to cover their actions.

5. **Historical Context:** Past actions and historical events involving the institution can influence current perceptions. For example, the many scandals and controversial decisions can have long-lasting effects on trust.

6. **Public Engagement:** Institutions that engage with the public, listen to concerns, and incorporate feedback are more likely to be viewed positively. The lack of transparent or meaningful engagement is what has led to feelings of alienation.

7. **Social and Cultural Factors:** Broader societal attitudes, including political polarization and cultural values, can influence how different groups perceive institutions. Trust levels may vary widely across different demographics.

8. **Performance and Effectiveness:** The perceived effectiveness of an institution in fulfilling its mandate can impact trust. If the DOJ is seen as successfully addressing crime and ensuring justice, it may foster greater trust. Unfortunately, they've been engaged in so many illegal activities and crimes against Americans themselves that they haven't done much to deter crime in American cities or against America.

9. **Legal and Ethical Standards:** Adherence to legal and ethical standards is crucial. Any perception of corruption, unethical behavior, or failure to uphold the law can lead to significant distrust. In the last 4 years, so much impropriety has been proven that distrust is all citizens have when it comes to the DOJ and FBI.

10. **Crisis Situations:** Events such as high-profile investigations, national crises, or significant legal rulings can temporarily alter public perception, either boosting or

undermining trust depending on the outcomes and responses. It's worse when they have a hand in such events and then use their power to cover up their covert actions.

The Department of Justice (DOJ) and the Federal Bureau of Investigation (FBI) have faced various accusations over the years regarding corrupt or unethical practices. Some have been proven and more are still yet to be shown to the world.

1. **Political Bias:** The DOJ and FBI have acted with political bias, particularly during high-profile investigations. Critics argue that certain investigations were influenced by political motivations.

2. **Surveillance Abuse:** The FBI has been criticized for its use of illegal surveillance techniques, including the application of the Foreign Intelligence Surveillance Act (FISA). Instances of improper surveillance or failure to follow proper procedures have led to accusations of overreach.

3. **Handling of the Clinton Email Investigation:** The DOJ and FBI faced scrutiny over the weak investigation into Hillary Clinton's use of a private email server during her tenure as Secretary of State. Accusations of favoritism and mishandling of the investigation were obvious.

4. **The Russia Investigation:** The investigation into Russian interference in the 2016 election, led by Special Counsel Robert Mueller, was proven to be a politically motivated witch hunt, leading to obvious claims of misconduct by the DOJ and FBI that still need to be addressed.

5. **Use of Informants:** The FBI has been criticized for its use of informants in various investigations, with accusations that some informants were not properly vetted or that their information was unreliable.

6. **Misconduct in the Lead-Up to the January 6 Capitol Riot:** Some have accused the FBI and DOJ of failing to adequately address intelligence regarding the potential for violence on January 6, 2021, leading to accusations of negligence. It's also been proven that they had undercover Agents there stirring up chaos in the crowd.

7. **Excessive Force and Civil Liberties Violations:** Both agencies have faced multiple allegations of excessive use of force and abuse in certain operations, as well as violations of civil liberties in their efforts to combat crime and terrorism.

These accusations often lead to public debates about accountability, transparency, and reform within these agencies.

Addressing concerns about the DOJ and FBI regarding abuse, overreach, corruption, and illegal activities is a complex issue that involves multiple strategies and reforms. Here are some approaches that could be used to obtain accountability and transparency within these agencies:

1. **Enhanced Oversight:** Establish independent oversight bodies that can monitor the actions of the DOJ and FBI, investigate allegations of misconduct, and provide recommendations for reforms.

2. **Whistleblower Protections:** Strengthen protections for whistleblowers to encourage individuals within these agencies to report misconduct without fear of retaliation.

3. **Transparency Measures:** Implement policies that require greater transparency in operations, including the release of documents related to investigations and the decision-making processes of the agencies.

4. **Legislative Reforms:** Advocate for legislative changes that impose stricter guidelines and limitations on surveillance practices, informant usage, and other controversial tactics employed by the agencies.

5. **Training and Education:** Provide comprehensive training for agents and officials on ethical practices, civil liberties, and the importance of maintaining public trust to foster a culture of accountability.

6. **Public Accountability:** Encourage regular public hearings and reports to hold leadership accountable for the actions of their agencies, allowing for public scrutiny and input.

7. **Judicial Checks:** Support robust judicial review of agency actions, ensuring that courts have the authority to challenge illegal or unethical practices.

8. **Community Engagement:** Foster relationships between law enforcement agencies and the communities they serve, encouraging dialogue and collaboration to build trust and reduce instances of overreach.

9. **Independent Investigations:** In cases of alleged misconduct, allow for independent investigations by external bodies to ensure impartiality and credibility.

10. **Media and Advocacy:** Encourage investigative journalism and advocacy organizations to shed light on issues within the DOJ and FBI, promoting public awareness and accountability.

Ultimately, a combination of these strategies, alongside transparency, strict oversight, accountability, and active civic engagement, can help ensure that the DOJ and FBI operate within their legal and ethical boundaries, maintaining the public's trust and upholding justice.

CHAPTER 3

GOVERNMENT OFFICIALS ARE SUPPOSED TO WORK FOR AMERICANS

Government officials in the United States are voted in and entrusted with the significant responsibility of serving the legal citizens. Their primary role is to represent the interests of the American public, ensuring that the needs and concerns of the U.S. communities are adequately addressed.

Government Officials should all have short terms with no way to lobby, rig elections, vote for themselves, raise or make laws for citizens but not themselves; they should be able to be fired at any time for crimes against America, the original Constitution, and their sworn oaths. They must be held to a higher standard.

These are some key ways they are supposed to work for U.S. citizens:

1. **Representation**: Officials, whether at the federal, state, or local level, are elected to represent the views and interests of their constituents. This means listening to the community, understanding their needs, and advocating for policies that reflect those priorities without any promises of financial gain.

2. **Legislation:** Government officials are responsible for creating laws that enhance the well-being of American citizens only. This includes drafting, debating, and voting on legislation that affects various aspects of daily life, such as healthcare, education, and public safety.

3. **Accountability**: Transparency and Accountability are crucial in governance. Officials must be answerable to the public and the justice system for their actions and decisions and not untouchable. Regular town hall meetings, open forums, and accessible communication channels are essential for maintaining this accountability. They should be subject to any and all laws as citizens and prosecuted for any corruption, tyranny, or law breaking.

4. **Service Delivery**: Government officials oversee the implementation of public services, ensuring that legal citizens have access to essential resources like education, healthcare, infrastructure, and social services. They must work to improve the efficiency and effectiveness of these services for Americans.

5. **Crisis Management**: In times of crisis, such as natural disasters or public health emergencies, officials are expected to lead response efforts, allocate resources, and

communicate effectively with the public to ensure safety and recovery. Officials should not have any vested or financial interests in any way that aid in the recovery of such emergencies.

6. **Community Engagement**: Building relationships with the community is vital. Officials should engage with American citizens through outreach programs, surveys, and community events to gather input and foster trust. They should not have any close ties to large corporations, organizations, foreign influences or institutions.

7. **Advocacy for Rights**: Officials are charged with protecting the rights of all legal American citizens, advocating for social justice, equity, and inclusion. They should work to dismantle barriers that prevent individuals from fully participating in society. Their job is to uphold the U.S. Constitution and not find ways to work around it for their own benefit or that of other influences.

8. **Fiscal Responsibility**: Managing public funds wisely is essential. Officials must ensure that taxpayer money is spent efficiently and effectively, focusing on projects and policies that benefit the community. The government should not have free range and access to American tax money and resources to do with as they please. There needs to be strong oversight and strict accountability for every penny, and it needs to be independently audited each year as they do with us with the IRS. The needs of America /Americans must always come first. Not one cent of American tax funds should be spent on foreign investments, infrastructure, or citizens without a 75% vote from American citizens.

In summary, government officials are meant to act as stewards of the American people, working diligently to create a better society for all legal U.S. citizens. Their effectiveness hinges on their ability to engage with the community, advocate for their needs, and uphold the principles of the Constitution, democracy, and accountability.

CHAPTER 4

ALL GOVERNMENT OFFICIALS SHOULD BE AUDITED YEARLY

The notion that politicians should be completely insulated from financial influences is rooted in the principle of integrity and accountability in governance. The idea is that no politician should receive any form of funding, gifts, assistance, or financial support from lobbyists, individuals, or corporations. This would effectively minimize conflicts of interest, ensuring that elected officials prioritize the public interest over private gains.

By eliminating these financial ties, we could foster a political landscape where decisions are made transparently and solely for the benefit of the American people. The presence of lobbyists often skews policies toward special interests, undermining democratic principles and eroding public trust. Therefore, a complete ban on funding from such entities would cultivate a more equitable and representative governance structure.

Additionally, instituting annual audits for politicians can enhance accountability. These audits would scrutinize their financial activities and lifestyle, confirming that their means align with their official salaries, just as the IRS does with regular citizens. This transparency can deter corruption and misuse of power, as officials would be aware that their financial dealings are subject to public scrutiny.

This dual approach—prohibiting financial support from external sources and implementing regular audits—can pave the way for a government that operates with greater integrity, prioritizing the needs of the public and enhancing trust in political institutions. Ultimately, it would empower American citizens by ensuring that their representatives are truly serving their interests, free from the undue influence of money or any other type of gifts/rewards.

How can these people have this astounding Net Worth on the Salaries they receive without Theft and Corruption?

Examples:

Nancy Pelosi: Salary - $223,000 / Net worth - $202,000,000
Mitch McConnell: Salary - $200,000 / Net Worth - $95,000,000
Chuck Schumer: Salary - $210,000 / Net Worth - $75,000,000
Elizabeth Warren: Salary - $285,000 / Net worth - $67,000,000

Alexandria Cortez: Salary - $174,000 / Net Worth - $29,000,000
Kamala Harris: Salary as Vice President of the United States is $235,100 per year. This salary is set by law for the position of Vice President. Net Worth - $7,000,000 as of 2023.
Joe Biden: Salary - is $400,000 per year. This salary is set by law and is the same for all U.S. presidents. In addition to the salary, the president also receives other benefits, such as a residence at the White House and an expense allowance. Net Worth - $9,000,000 as of 2023 (Does not include all the illegal money laundering from Ukraine and China).

The answer is...They Can't. This is clear and present corruption.

There are a few reasons why politicians may not be subject to more extensive auditing to determine how they accumulate wealth on a government salary. Most of it is because they know how to hide each other's crimes and thievery through their corrupt system.

1. **Lack of clear legal requirements:** Unfortunately, there are generally no specific laws or regulations that mandate routine auditing or extensive financial disclosure requirements for elected officials beyond basic financial reporting. The requirements can vary by jurisdiction, but seem to favor hiding or protecting politicians from being audited.

2. **Potential conflicts of interest:** Subjecting politicians to more invasive audits could be seen as politically motivated or a conflict of interest, as the auditors and

oversight mechanisms may ultimately report to the very politicians being audited. However, every politician should be subject to the same level of audits and financial oversight to prevent corruption.

3. **Privacy concerns:** There are often concerns about infringing on the privacy and personal financial information of public officials, even if they are in positions of power, but they need to be under the same level of scrutiny as every U.S. citizen, if not more.

4. **Enforcement challenges:** Implementing and enforcing comprehensive auditing programs for all elected officials can be logistically and resource-intensive, especially at higher levels of government, because they control the system to benefit their illegal activities and ways to hide money.

5. **Lack of political will:** There may be a lack of political will to implement stricter financial oversight, as politicians may be reluctant to subject themselves and their colleagues to increased scrutiny. It's a game they play; if I get caught, you get caught, so they all hide each other's secrets and crimes.

6. **Existing financial disclosure requirements:** Many politicians are required to file financial disclosure forms that provide some insight into their assets and income sources. However, as we can clearly see, these disclosures don't always paint a complete picture.

That said, there have been calls for greater financial transparency's and accountability for elected officials in the U.S.. But the balance between oversight and privacy remains an ongoing debate.

D.O.G.E.

Department of Oversight and Government Efficiency

Many presidents in the past have talked about controlling government spending to get people on their side during their campaign runs, but at the same time, they're involved in receiving and distributing so much of those funds. Well, now, we finally have a President in Donald Trump, who has appointed a "Special Government Employee" in Elon Musk (who does NOT draw a Government salary) and is exposing the wasteful spending of our American Tax dollars. Saying "Wasteful Spending" is the nice way of saying that this corrupt, tyrannical criminal ring of government officials is not involved in "government spending" but is blatantly "STEALING" from us ALL.

The Department of Oversight and Government Efficiency is an initiative of the 2025 Donald Trump administration that is tasked with reducing federal spending.

President Trump has issued several executive orders involving DOGE: On January 20, executive order 14158, "Establishing and Implementing the President's 'Department of Government Efficiency." Their duty is to investigate, locate, and stop the illegal and unethical theft/spending of American tax dollars that is going out to numerous NGO's and money laundering schemes created by the U.S. criminal government enterprise.

Amazingly and sadly, so many of the American people have been brainwashed for so long that they still don't see the evil of what the government has been doing by extorting their hard-earned money and then using it to enrich themselves and their corporate entities. All this while we're having a hard time paying bills, feeding our families, and keeping businesses open. The benefit of D.O.G.E. is that they are EXPOSING a huge amount of scams, fraudulent businesses, and flat out theft of the citizen's living funds.

How can these people be okay with the government misusing your hard-earned money? Do you not want to know how people like Stacey Abrams were gifted $7 Billion dollars of YOUR money or how we've been funding government officials with moderate salaries who become multi-millionaires during their relatively short terms in office, Transexual Operas in Foreign Countries or paying billions for condoms in foreign countries etc? If that's not a concern of yours, then you deserve to lose everything that you own and work for because YOU are a Huge Part of the Problem!

How about all the Government employees who have taxpayer-funded credit cards for their lunches and who knows what else they use them for; this is absolutely ridiculous; if I have to pay for my lunch, then they should as well…So, how do you complain about DOGE who is exposing the crime syndicate aka the U.S. Government who is draining you of any bit of money that you make and then watching you suffer as you struggle to survive while filling their pockets with your cash? That sounds like a bunch of stupid, brainwashed idiots to me! How about, if you support how this government has been operating then **"You Give Them Yours, and I'll Keep Mine"!**

D.O.G.E. (the Department of Oversight and Government Efficiency) has made significant strides in uncovering huge amounts of government waste in numerous sectors. They have identified billions if not Trillions of dollars in wasteful spending across many government programs and agencies. This includes inefficiencies, redundant programs, and misallocated resources such as NGO's.

Some specific findings have found huge issues with excessive expenditures on contracts, underutilized assets, and funds allocated to programs that are no longer effective for the United States. The ongoing audits and evaluations by D.O.G.E. aim to promote transparency and accountability in government spending, with the ultimate goal of reallocating resources to more impactful initiatives that actually benefit the American people and this Country rather than all the foreign interests of the criminals in charge of and laundering OUR money without any oversight or accountability.

The Bullshit Reasons why government officials may not be Audited as regularly as private citizens:

1. **Transparency and Accountability:** Many governments have established systems for transparency and accountability, such as financial disclosures and ethics regulations. While these systems may not be as rigorous as annual audits, they aim to provide a level of oversight that is easily overcome and/or bypassed for the proper people.

2. **Resource Allocation:** They say that conducting thorough audits of all government officials annually would require significant resources and manpower. This shouldn't be a problem since the IRS does it for every working American citizen each year.... Governments seem to prioritize audits of certain departments or officials based on their positions or status, which should be completely illegal.

3. **Legal Framework:** The legal requirements for auditing government officials should be the same as for every other citizen in America and shouldn't, but can vary significantly between jurisdictions. Government officials create laws so that some places may lack the necessary laws to mandate regular audits, while others may have established guidelines that focus on specific roles or situations.

4. **Political Sensitivity:** Auditing government officials can be politically sensitive and possibly hazardous to the health of those doing the auditing. These politicians have so much to cover up that there may be concerns about the potential for audits to be used as political tools, leading to resistance from officials or political parties.

5. **Public Trust:** In some cases, there might be an assumption that public officials should be trusted to act in the public's best interest, but unfortunately, we've seen through the work of D.O.G.E. That every U.S. Politician should be extensively audited every year!

While there are supposedly mechanisms for oversight and accountability, the effectiveness and frequency of these measures are very weak and can vary widely depending on the political party or politician.

CHAPTER 5
PERSONAL RESPONSIBILITY
YOU PAY FOR YOURS AND I'LL PAY FOR MINE

The idea that each individual should be responsible for themselves and

their own family is rooted in the belief in personal sacrifice, accountability, and self-sufficiency.

This perspective emphasizes the importance of individual effort and the notion that everyone should work toward their own financial stability without relying on others. Nobody should be forced to work, sacrifice, or take care of another without their own desire to do so. If you want the things that others have, get your ass up, get out there and work for it and earn what you want the same way that others are doing! If you want that house or car, work for it; if you want to go on vacation, get your hair and nails done, or anything else, work for it; if you want to eat at that restaurant, work for it and if you want to have children, then you damn well better be able to afford them on your own, so go out and work for it!

Advocates of this viewpoint argue that when people are solely responsible for their own financial well-being, it fosters a sense of independence and encourages individuals to strive for success through hard work and determination. This approach can lead to a stronger work ethic and a greater appreciation for the resources one has, as each person directly reaps the rewards of their labor.

Moreover, this philosophy suggests that the government or society should not be expected to provide financial support through taxes or other means unless individuals choose to contribute voluntarily. The belief is that individuals should have the freedom to allocate their resources as they see fit, without being compelled to support others unless they wish to do so out of personal conviction or charity. This system will also stop the government from misappropriating your hard-earned tax dollars and forcing hard-working individuals from supporting the lazy, freeloaders, illegal aliens, and other foreign interests.

Critics of this viewpoint may argue that it overlooks the complexities of social inequality and the varying circumstances that can impact a person's ability to support themselves. They might contend that a safety net is necessary to ensure that all members of society have access to basic needs, especially in times of crisis.

Ultimately, the debate surrounding personal responsibility versus societal support is multifaceted. While the idea of "you pay for yours, and I'll pay for mine" promotes individualism and self-reliance, it also raises important questions about the role of community and the collective responsibility to care for one another, especially in an increasingly interconnected world.

Plain and Simple
I, nor many people that I know with common sense do NOT want to work hard every day just to fund anybody or any entity that is not of our own choosing!

We work to support ourselves and our Families, not foreigners, foreign interests or programs, lazy able-bodied Adult Americans who know how to work the Welfare system, constantly pregnant women whom can't even afford to fund themselves, or ANY other program or person out there that my Extorted money goes too. I will work and pay for myself and my family as each individual should do. For that, I will earn and deserve anything I get for myself and won't be responsible for anybody or relied on by anybody else.

Work for what you want and you get what you work for. Remove and or dramatically limit assistance programs and get people out there working for a better life. That alone will remove the need for the false need of immigrant workers in America.

Assistance Programs for Americans:

1. Food Assistance: Supplemental Nutrition Assistance Program (SNAP): Provides eligible low-income individuals and families with funds to purchase food.

Women, Infants, and Children (WIC): Offers nutrition assistance to pregnant women, new mothers, and young children.

2. Housing Assistance: Section 8 Housing Choice Voucher Program: Helps low-income families afford housing in the private market.

Public Housing: Provides rental housing for low-income families, the elderly, and persons with disabilities.

3. Healthcare Programs: Medicaid: Offers health coverage to eligible low-income individuals and families.

Children's Health Insurance Program (CHIP): Provides health coverage to children in families with incomes too high to qualify for Medicaid.

4. Financial Assistance: Temporary Assistance for Needy Families (TANF): Provides financial assistance and support services to low-income families.

Unemployment Insurance: Offers temporary financial assistance to workers who have lost their jobs.

5. Education and Workforce Development: Pell Grants: Federal grants for low-income college students.

Job Training Programs: Various initiatives aimed at helping individuals gain skills and employment.

Assistance Programs for Undocumented Immigrants:

1. Emergency Services: Some states and localities provide emergency medical services regardless of immigration status.

2. Food Assistance: Local Food Banks and Pantries: Many food banks do not require proof of citizenship and provide food to those in need.

3. Legal Aid: Nonprofit organizations often provide legal assistance to help undocumented immigrants navigate their status and rights.

4. Education: Some states allow undocumented immigrants to attend public schools and, in some cases, offer in-state tuition rates for higher education.

5. Healthcare: Some states have programs that provide limited health services to undocumented residents, particularly for children and pregnant women.

6. Community-Based Support: Various nonprofit organizations and community groups offer resources, support, and advocacy for undocumented immigrants.

A good way to stop the abuse of the welfare system is to have term limits on assistance, encourage people to better themselves, and stop giving them a better living than those who work for a living. If they have less but want more, they can work for it, just as we all have to do on a daily basis. Not one cent of my hard-earned money should be allocated to funding another grown adult or their family without my direct desire to do so. And for that, I do support an individual's right to give of their own money to whatever cause they see fit; just don't allocate my money to something that I don't agree with.

It's funny how there are so many fools/good-hearted people who want these programs and believe that we should have these programs because every human deserves a good life, and yet they are NOT willing to be the ones to house the homeless, illegal immigrants or provide their own funds for any of these people who are on assistance programs! Funny how that works! They should "Step Up and Support" those in need so we can Stop the Career Choice/Abuse of Public Assistance!

<u>*No More Handouts!*</u>

Everyone Should Work for Their Own Family and A Better Life.

CHAPTER 6

FUNDING FOREIGN NATIONS

I do not believe that the U.S. should be funding other nations in any way, not financially, not with food, not with housing, and definitely not with weapons. The United States is currently $35 trillion in debt. If we have so much money to fund other nations, then Americans are paying way too much in taxes. We work to support ourselves, our own families, and our country, not foreign interests with our tax dollars. America should always come first, especially when it comes to spending our hard-earned tax dollars. Before giving and or supporting any other country, not one U.S. Veteran should be homeless or hungry, not one U.S. Family should be homeless and hungry, not one U.S. City or Town should be in ruins, and the debt should be paid off.

For others, the debate over funding foreign nations with American tax dollars versus addressing domestic needs is complex and often contentious. Here are some key points that are usually brought up and could be considered:

1. **Global Stability**: Supporting foreign nations can help maintain global stability and reduce the likelihood of conflict, which can ultimately benefit the U.S. by preventing wars and humanitarian crises that could lead to greater expenses down the line.

2. **Economic Interests:** I am obviously against foreign aid, but many foreign aid programs support U.S. economic interests. By investing in developing economies, the U.S. can foster markets for American goods, which can possibly lead to job creation domestically.

3. **Humanitarian Commitment**: The U.S. has a long-standing tradition of humanitarian aid (except for our own citizens). Helping those in need can reflect American values and commitment to global citizenship and can also enhance the U.S.'s reputation abroad, which is usually besmirched by many nations, including those that we help.

4. **Interconnected Challenges**: Many actual or fictional challenges, such as climate change, pandemics, and terrorism, are global issues that require international cooperation. Addressing these issues abroad can help mitigate their effects on the U.S. This, of course, does not include funding current or future terrorist organizations, paying for, creating and releasing viruses to manipulate a pandemic or any other disgusting acts....

5. **Strategic Alliances**: Providing aid can strengthen diplomatic relationships and foster alliances that are beneficial for national security. However, the aid must benefit both parties and not just the other country, as it happens with most of our so-called alliances.

While it's crucial to address domestic issues, proponents of foreign aid argue that a balanced approach can ultimately serve both American interests and those of the global community. The challenge lies in finding the right balance between both countries benefiting, investing in domestic needs, and engaging in international responsibilities.

Americans are homeless, starving, being over-taxed, dealing with ridiculous costs of living increases and our country is going to shit while the government gives billions of dollars in aid to foreigners! As much as i want it to stop and believe it should be stopped, Stopping all foreign aid might have several significant consequences, both domestically and internationally:

1. **Global Stability**: Many countries rely on foreign aid for stability, governance, and humanitarian needs. Though we should first concentrate on our own country's needs, cutting off aid could lead to increased instability, which might result in conflicts or humanitarian crises that could possibly spill over borders and affect U.S. security.

2. **Diplomatic Relations**: Foreign aid is often a tool of diplomacy. Halting it could strain relations with allied nations, making it harder to collaborate on issues like trade and security.

3. **Economic Impact**: U.S. foreign aid supports American jobs in sectors such as agriculture, healthcare, and construction. A reduction in aid could negatively impact those industries that rely on international contracts and partnership agreements.

4. **Humanitarian Consequences**: Many people around the world depend on U.S. aid for food, health care, and education. Stopping aid could exacerbate poverty and suffering in vulnerable populations. It's just too bad that our government will feed, house, and provide medical care to foreigners for free but will over-charge and or withhold those same things from American citizens.

5. **Public Health Risks**: Many global health initiatives funded by U.S. aid help control diseases that can cross borders. Stopping this funding might hinder efforts to combat pandemics and other health crises. This is where closed borders and strict medical checks on all foreigners entering our country is needed.

6. **Reputation Damage**: The U.S. has historically positioned itself as a leader in humanitarian efforts for everyone except those Americans paying the bills through over-taxation. Ending foreign aid could damage its global reputation and influence, leading to a loss of soft power.

7. **Migration Pressure**: Increased instability and poverty in aid-dependent countries could lead to higher rates of migration toward the U.S., creating additional domestic challenges. Stronger laws, border walls, and protection could protect us from migrant invaders.

While the argument for prioritizing domestic spending is valid, the potential repercussions of cutting off foreign aid warrant careful consideration. Balancing domestic needs with global responsibilities is a complex issue that requires thoughtful debate and policy-making.

This List is the Real Reason for Funding Foreign Countries

CHAPTER 7

SYSTEMATIC CORRUPTION BY THE U.S. GOVERNMENT

Systematic corruption within the U.S. government is running rampant and in plain view of the American people. It can be viewed through various lenses, including campaign finance, lobbying, regulatory capture, and the influence of special interest groups. All of this needs to be stopped, the corrupt officials need to be arrested and prosecuted. Nobody is supposed to be above the law; there aren't two sets of laws between American Citizens and American Politicians, and therefore, if we'd get arrested, publicly bashed, prosecuted, and jailed for a crime, so should they and their co-conspirators.

Furthermore, they should be removed from office, be unable to ever hold office or any official title again, lose any and all financial wealth, property and items illegally gained from such crimes, lose any licenses that were obtained, as well as pensions and personal protection. I believe that if they had the same accountability and oversight that normal citizens have with them facing the same or worse consequences, there would be little to no conflicts of interest, corruption, and tyrannical behavior. This type of corruption breeds conflict between doing what's right for the citizen's future of this country and doing for themselves or their financial backers.

<u>Some Clear Types of Political Corruption that Need to be Stopped</u>

1. **Campaign Finance**: The role of money in politics is significant. The Supreme Court's decision in Citizens United v. FEC (2010) allowed for unlimited contributions to independent political expenditures, leading to the rise of Super PACs. This situation has enabled wealthy individuals and corporations to exert considerable influence over political candidates and parties, often prioritizing their interests over those of the general public.

2. **Lobbying**: Lobbyists represent special interest groups, including corporations, unions, and non-profits, aiming to influence legislation and policy. This creates a potential conflict of interest, as elected officials may prioritize the desires of their contributors over their constituents. The sheer volume of lobbying dollars spent annually indicates the extent of this influence.

3. **Regulatory Capture**: This occurs when regulatory agencies are dominated by the industries they are supposed to regulate. For instance, the revolving door phenomenon—where government officials transition to high-paying jobs in the industries they once regulated—can lead to policies that favor businesses over public welfare.

4. **Transparency and Accountability**: Lack of transparency in government dealings and insufficient mechanisms for accountability can perpetuate corruption. Whistleblower protections are crucial, but they are often inadequate, deterring individuals from coming forward about unethical practices. Such protection should have been given to Edward Snowden, the former NSA contractor who became a "Whistleblower" and was ostracized for trying to warn/protect the American people.

5. **Inequality in Representation**: Government Officials were elected to represent all of their constituents equally and swore an oath to do so. The interests of marginalized communities often go unheard, as systemic corruption tends to prioritize the voices of those with financial power. This can lead to policies that exacerbate social and economic inequalities.

6. **Public Trust**: Systematic corruption erodes public trust in government institutions. When citizens perceive their government as corrupt, they may disengage from the political process, further entrenching the power of those who benefit from the system. You can't trust a government that swore to represent you but puts as much distance between themselves and you, passes laws against American prosperity and continues to tax you into poverty, all while lining their own pockets with money and representing those financial partners and special interests that back them

The U.S. Government has become way too big, which has led to their Tyrannical overreach, policies, over-taxation, and laws that are made only for the citizens and not themselves. Ending systematic corruption requires comprehensive reforms, including campaign finance reform, stricter lobbying regulations, and efforts to enhance transparency, accountability, and public engagement in the political process.

It's obvious who in the government has been getting wealthy by stealing from the U.S. Citizens because they are the ones who are yelling the loudest and fighting back against D.O.G.E.! Their illegal money streams are being discovered and cut off by the program. We, the citizens/victims of these fraudsters, are still waiting for them to be indicted and sent to jail.

If they weren't doing anything wrong and if they truly cared about America, then they wouldn't have any problem with DOGE searching out government waste and all the illegal/fraudulent activities that have been going on. But they do have a problem with it because they are the criminals that are stealing our money and are being exposed for their illegal business/government practices.

AutoPen usage in the Biden Administration

In March 2025, it was found that at least six important government documents (Presidential Pardons) were supposedly signed by Joe Biden; it was discovered that these documents were signed while sleepy Joe was on vacation and done by "AutoPen." Who knows how many other important government documents were signed by unknown individuals using this AutoPen and knowingly or unknowingly representing Joe Biden and his dysfunctional administration?

CHAPTER 8

ACCOUNTABILITY AND TRANSPARENCY IN GOVERNMENT

Individuals can and should take several to advocate for transparency and accountability in government:

1. **Educate Yourself and Others**: Understanding the issues surrounding government transparency is crucial. Share knowledge through discussions, social media, or community events to raise awareness about the importance of transparency and its impact on democracy.

2. **Engage with Local Government**: Attend town hall meetings, city council sessions, or public hearings. Ask questions, voice concerns, and encourage other community members to participate. Engaging directly with local officials helps hold them accountable. They must be working for our community's best interests and not their own at the City, State, and Federal levels.

3. **Support Transparency Legislation**: Advocate for laws that promote transparency, such as open records laws, whistleblower protections, and campaign finance reforms. Support candidates who prioritize transparency and accountability in their platforms.

4. **Utilize Freedom of Information Act (FOIA) Requests**: Familiarize yourself with the FOIA and state-level open records laws. Individuals can file requests to access government documents, fostering transparency and accountability.

5. **Join Advocacy Groups**: Participate in or support organizations that promote government transparency, such as Common Cause, the Sunlight Foundation, or local watchdog groups. These organizations often lead campaigns, provide resources, and mobilize citizens.

6. **Promote Open Data Initiatives**: Advocate for government agencies to adopt open data practices, making public datasets easily accessible. This can enhance transparency and enable citizens to analyze government activities.

7. **Use Social Media and Digital Platforms**: Share information and raise awareness about transparency issues through social media. Online campaigns can mobilize support and bring attention to specific concerns.

8. **Encourage Civic Engagement**: Promote voter registration and participation in elections. An informed and active electorate is essential for demanding transparency from elected officials.

9. **Report Corruption or Misconduct**: If you witness corruption or unethical behavior, report it to the appropriate authorities or media outlets. Whistleblower protections can help shield those who come forward. <u>**STOP THEM NOW!**</u> If you allow corruption, it'll only get worse. But if we all stand up and make them all accessible and accountable, then we can have a government with integrity that we, the American citizens, can trust!

10. **Collaborate with Journalists**: Investigative journalism not from the "Mainstream Media" plays a critical role in uncovering corruption. Support local journalism and collaborate with reporters who focus on transparency issues and who aren't a dirty part of the narrative.

By taking these actions, individuals can contribute to a culture of transparency and accountability in government, fostering a more informed and engaged citizenry while strengthening ourselves and slowing the rise of our increasingly corrupt and tyrannical government.

The U.S. Government has committed so many atrocities against its own American people, and they all need to be accountable for the mass losses of American lives. They kill us off with nothing a second thought for their agenda and, pass it off as some "False Flag" event and never take responsibility for their actions. That must all end!

Morning blog! No wonder the judge wanted the planes turned around.

Ever wonder what drives a federal judge to order planes full of illegal immigrants, whom are gang members such as MS13 and Tren De Aragua, to turn back? Maybe it's because his wife runs an abortion NGO funded by USAID, and his daughter Katherine works for Partners for Justice — a group that serves legal support to those very same criminals, thanks to 76% of their cash flow coming from Uncle Sam!

This organization is like an anti-deportation cheer squad and even boasts about having knocked off 5,000 years of prison time since 2018.

So, when investigative journalist Laura Loomer started connecting these dots, the judges wife Katherine suddenly ghosted her social media accounts like linked in, faster than a bad Tinder date!

This raises a big, blinking ethical alarm. According to the U.S. Judges' Code of Conduct, judges should recuse themselves if a close relative might benefit from their decisions. Yet here we are, with a judge whose rulings are practically aligned with his daughter's paycheck. National security? More like family vacation! Talk about mixing business with, uh, "personal" interests! Nothing to see here folks 👀

CHAPTER 9
FALSE ADVERTISING LAWS - WHAT HAPPENED TO PRODUCT INTEGRITY

What happened to the "False Advertising" laws? What happened to accountability and consumers being able to sue a company for giving false testimony about their products and selling their "Falsely Promoted Products" to unsuspecting consumers? How are they allowed to flood the markets with the next big fad and claim to have the purest quality and best name-branded product on the market with nothing but false claims?

Every products says the same thing, like "if you take this product for 30 days, you'll get these results/benefits, everything is scientifically tested and designed, our products are 3rd party tested, they also use Joe Rogan or some other influencers voice to say how great something is. But most products are a placebo, empty powder in plastic capsules, over-amplified caffeine pills or powders, and empty flavored powders with a very minimal amount of actual product in the mix. They have little to no health or described benefits at all, and some could also be dangerous in one way or another. Plain and simple, we're wasting our hard-earned money on "Fake Junk" that needs to be strictly regulated!

False advertising laws are supposed to exist to protect consumers from misleading claims about products, but enforcing these laws can be challenging. Many companies use vague language or general claims that can be difficult to legally contest. Additionally and unfortunately, the burden of proof often falls on the consumer to demonstrate that a product is indeed ineffective or misleading.

In recent years, there have been increased calls for stricter regulations and more transparency in marketing, particularly regarding health and wellness products. Some jurisdictions have begun to crack down on misleading claims, especially those that lack scientific backing. The problem is, they all say the same crap about being scientifically designed and tested, but we all know that anyone can identify as a scientist these days, and when they're getting paid to say the right thing about a product, it usually comes out scientifically backed!

However, the prevalence of placebo effects and subjective experiences can make it hard to label a product as outright ineffective, even if scientific evidence is lacking. Consumers should approach health claims critically and look for products that provide clear, verifiable evidence of their effectiveness, such as peer-reviewed studies or endorsements from reputable health organizations.

Companies often employ various tactics in misleading advertising to attract consumers and promote their products. Here are some common strategies. Here are a few disturbing examples of how they skate the law to rip you off:

1. **Vague Language**: Using ambiguous terms like "clinically proven" or "natural" without specifying what that means can mislead consumers about the actual benefits.

2. **Exaggerated Claims**: Making bold promises about a product's effectiveness that are not backed by solid evidence. For example, claiming significant weight loss without mentioning the need for diet and exercise.

3. **Testimonials and Anecdotes**: Relying on personal stories or testimonials from users, which can be compelling but do not constitute scientific proof of effectiveness.

4. **Hidden Disclaimers**: Including small print or disclaimers that are difficult to read or notice, which can downplay the actual risks or limitations of a product.

5. **Imagery and Emotional Appeal**: Using attractive visuals or emotional triggers to create a favorable impression of a product, even if it doesn't deliver on the promises made.

6. **Comparison with Competitors**: Making misleading comparisons with other products to imply superiority without providing context or fair evidence.

7. **Limited-Time Offers**: Creating a sense of urgency with phrases like "limited time only" to pressure consumers into quick decisions without considering the product's true value.

8. **Omitting Negative Information**: Failing to mention potential side effects or downsides associated with a product while emphasizing only the benefits.

9. **Over-reliance on Scientific Jargon**: Using complex scientific terms or concepts that may confuse consumers into believing a product is more effective or credible than it truly is.

10. **Creating False Scarcity**: Suggesting that a product is in limited supply to encourage immediate purchase decisions.

Being aware of these tactics can help consumers make more informed choices and recognize potentially misleading advertising.

COMMON TYPES OF FALSE ADVERTISING

- Mislabeling
- Bait-and-Switch
- Failure to Disclose
- Product Disparagement & Trademark Infringement
- Puffery
- Unscientific Claims
- False Reviews and Testimonials
- Hidden Fees

It's very bothersome to spend your hard-earned money on cleverly advertised products where you are expecting to get a certain quality of food or other product(s) and then receive a sad fraction of what you've seen and desired. The quality isn't there, the look and appeal aren't there, and you don't get the results that you were told you'd get, which, for the most part, is satisfaction. It's hard to feel satisfied when you don't get what you've seen pay for. Unfortunately, almost all companies have lost their sense of integrity and have traded their product quality for profit. Just look at the Mc D's Big M. It is at this time 40% smaller than it used to be and yet the price has quadrupled, so you're getting a sad fraction of what used to be advertised and for a lot more money. Where's the value in that? Far too many companies are doing the same; you get poor quality and a lot less product for a lot more money. Fast-food chicken facilities are some of the worst as the chicken wings or body parts that we consume used to be from mature-sized chickens, and now they're so small that it's as though they're being prepped for consumption shortly after birth.

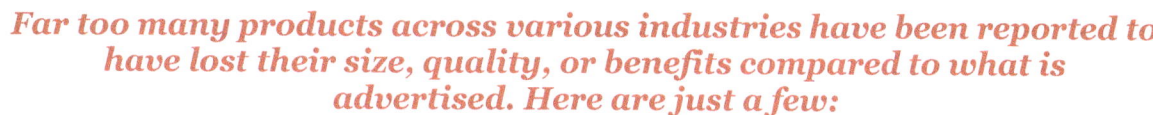

Far too many products across various industries have been reported to have lost their size, quality, or benefits compared to what is advertised. Here are just a few:

1. **Snack Foods:** Many consumers have noticed that popular snack products, such as chips and cookies, have reduced their package sizes while keeping the prices the same or higher. This practice is often referred to as "**shrinkflation**."

2. **Laundry Detergents:** Some brands have reformulated their products, reducing the concentration of active cleaning ingredients by adding mostly water, leading to less effective cleaning. Customers have reported needing to use more detergent to achieve the same results.

3. **Cosmetics and Skincare Products:** There have been instances where beauty products, like moisturizers and serums, have changed their formulations or sizes, leading to dissatisfaction among users regarding effectiveness.

4. **Cereal Brands:** Many breakfast cereals have undergone changes in size and formulation. Customers often notice that the same box is a lot smaller and contains fewer servings than before.

5. **Fast Food Portions:** Fast-food chains have all reduced portion sizes and food quality while maintaining or even increasing prices. This is a reason for their dissatisfaction with the diminished value of the meal(s).

6. **Beverages:** Soft drink companies have occasionally reduced the size of their cans or bottles while keeping the price steady, which has upset consumers expecting the same amount of product.

7. **Electronics:** Products like smartphones and laptops may advertise improved features but can sometimes have reduced build quality or battery life compared to earlier models.

8. **Clothing Brands:** Many clothing lines have faced criticism for inconsistencies in sizing, where the same size may fit differently across different styles or collections, leading to confusion and dissatisfaction.

9. **Vehicles:** My 2018 Toyota Tacoma had way more features than the 2023 model that I bought for more money. So here I had a newer vehicle with fewer features such as GPS systems, side view mirror blind spot indicators, Reverse mode traffic alert system, etc. Within three months, I traded the truck in for a GMC with all the features that I was missing. This is something that is happening all over; the vehicles are removing features of newer models while raising the prices.

These examples illustrate the importance of consumer awareness and advocacy for transparency in product marketing and quality.

CHAPTER 10

AMERICAN LAWS

The laws of the United States enslave us to our Politicians. They have written themselves into absolute power over its citizens.

So Breaking the Law is Against the Law Unless You're the one Making the Law!

I find it very disturbing that Most of you American Citizens have accepted that you are the subservient slaves of the United States Government!

As a child, I learned both the easy way and the hard way that my actions have consequences. I try and relay that message to the children that I train as a life lesson so that, hopefully they'll make the right decisions.

But how can any of us believe in the law when those in Government who are making the laws are the biggest and most frequent breakers of the law?

Why should any of us follow the laws of this Country when members of Congress and other Government Officials are so Corrupt? They lie, cheat, steal, and even kill...It's Law for All or Law for None, regardless of your "Elected" position!

These nasty Politicians are destroying our Country and our Future! They are Showing our Children that the way to get ahead is to give head and the way to stay in Power is to lie, cheat, steal, and kill....History has not been learned; our system is fatally flawed, and many great and powerful Nations before us have fallen following this same path!

They continue to take away everything that this country was founded on - Freedoms, Money, Happiness, Pursuit of Happiness. They continue to Create New Laws, New Fees, New Taxes, New Regulations, and more. Soon, they'll have a tax rate of 75 to 90% where you'll die working, and all your money will go to the Master Government! None for you, your family, for food, for bills or anything you may need or enjoy in life! They want to and will control you!

EXAMPLE:
9/11 (inside job or not) caused many deaths on American soil, and our Government used that event to create many new restrictions and laws to forgo our freedoms of privacy and much more. In 2020, a flu-like virus (COVID-19) was created and pushed onto the people, and with that, they have created many new avenues of control over your lives and continue to force their agendas upon us! YOU ARE NO LONGER IN CONTROL OF YOUR LIVES!

EXAMPLE:

I've talked to five different people who called the State to confirm that their Presidential votes had been counted. They were told YES, but when they asked whom their vote was counted towards, they were told that their own votes were confidential and would not be told whom their votes were counted for! What kind of shit is that? It's my fucking vote!!!

EXAMPLE: Nancy Pelosi instructs everyone to stay home, yet she gets caught getting her hair done. Her moronic nephew Gavin Newsom instructs all Californians to stay home and mask up, yet he is caught at a party (with no mask), etc. etc.

EXAMPLE: A Presidential election has been grossly corrupted by many facets of an opposing party and their followers counting the votes, mail delivery personnel, and others...

EXAMPLE:
A former President and his wife (Clinton) are responsible for multiple Homicides that cover up their Corruption, Greed, and Illegal Activities. The only thing that is being done about it is people making jokes and memes.

EXAMPLE:
John Legend, his wife, and many Hollywood Stars have their names on the list of people who have committed atrocities on the island of Jeffrey Epstein, and yet none of them have been prosecuted or even brought up on charges!

There are so many more examples, but I'd be here all night, and you get the picture! Soon you'll Have Nothing, you'll Be Nothing, and our Once Great Country will only exist in the History Books of the Future!

By Tyson Johnson / November 19, 2020

A country ran by Tyranny can only see Failure.

We must Stand and Fight for our Freedoms, Pursuit of Happiness, Prosperity, Liberty, and the Justice that we deserve.

The idea to have A Government Of, By, and For the People has been lost...

America is England all over again, but many times worse, except there is nowhere else for us to go! So we must Stand and Fight this Tyrannical Government and Eliminate them and their Greed, Corruption, and gross Over-Taxation.

We must Stand and Rise Up again until the Sheep become the Wolves...

Our Government Demands Loyalty, Taxes, and Obedience yet offers nothing to its own Citizens while giving everything to Foreigners, Refugees, and Themselves.

You must think of your ancestors who helped raise this country, your lives that you currently live, your children, and the future of your family and its name. Are you willing to give it all up?

They have been slowly increasing their power over you while taking away your freedoms, rights, and privileges as Americans more and more.

Are you Free Americans ready to give up everything? Your freedom, your rights, your property, your land, your estates, your dreams, your identity,

Do you not think that many Foreign Enemies aren't just waiting and watching the weakened and self-destructing United States destroy itself from within? Do you not think that at the right moment, they won't launch an attack to take over this land and destroy us all?

CHAPTER 11

AMERICA FIRST

Have we all Forgotten our own American Citizens who are Homeless and Jobless?

Shame on you American Politicians, Shame on you American Citizens, Shame on you Illegal (aliens, human beings, or occupants of America), Shame on you Starbucks and any other business that thinks protesting, marching, or giving aid to refugees or illegal foreign invaders is the humane thing to do when you have closed your eyes and hearts to the thousands of American Citizens right here in your own country! How about Starbucks hiring 10,000 U.S. (Jobless) Veterans instead of refugees? How can you say that you truly care and believe in human rights to live free and prosperous when all you're doing is closing your eyes to your problems here at home just to focus on external problems? How will bringing in more misplaced refugees benefit them or our country? Our Government can't or won't even take care of our own American Veterans who are homeless, hungry, and jobless, but yet it can support thousands of refugees? Or what about the "True Native American" people who are fighting against "Big Oil" just to preserve their clean water and lands? Are there multi-thousands of you marching for them? NO! But you'll protest and march for thousands of people to come here and occupy space we don't have, soak up services designed for needy Americans, and be given jobs that weren't given to jobless American Citizens?

Tell me, when will you fight, protest, and march for these people, your people, who are also human beings and actual citizens of these united states of america?

So many activists with so much misguided passion. So many people who fail to go to work and keep the American economy progressing just so they can pretend to care about other human beings not being allowed to over-crowd an already crowded country. **Where is that same passion for our own American citizens who are Homeless, Hungry, and Jobless? Should we not help them first? Should we not build a strong foundation at home before reaching out to aid others?**

How is it that you're all fighting for a better America while destroying American businesses, causing chaos, waving foreign flags on American soil, breaking American laws, and burning the American Flag? That doesn't sound like people wanting to be Americans to me!

So many activists are against building a wall to prevent the illegal occupation of our own country from a country (Mexico) that has their own heavily guarded wall against a bordering country to their south (Guatemala)! You claim it's racist, but how can the law be racist when there are legal ways and options for people to enter America, but

48

they choose to do it illegally? Try illegally crossing a border in North Korea, Iran, or many other countries, and you get severe punishments, not citizen tax-payer-funded benefits.

None of your excuses will make sense, such as they have family here because if they entered America illegally, then they are criminals as well and should be deported! **Immigration Enforcement is a LAW issue, not a RACE issue!**

You can't make excuses for breaking the law, and just because there are an estimated 12+ million illegal "human beings" currently in America doesn't mean that it's okay to break the law and that they should be able to stay. With that way of thinking, if 12 million Americans decided that they didn't agree with a law like "murder," would it be ok for them to all just be allowed to do it? Either the law is the law and should be enforced, or we remove all laws and see how fast this country is overrun and destroyed. It's not racist to stop one race from raping, murdering, or robbing from another race, just like it's not racist to stop the hordes or illegal "human beings" from illegally entering our country and draining our Government services! **Either you have a Nation of laws, or you don't.** Just because you don't like the man in charge, "President Trump," who is finally enforcing those laws, doesn't mean you should not obey the law. In the past, Presidents Reagan, Clinton, and Obama had the same agenda, and you all cheered them for it. The difference is that two of the three only lied to you about their agendas just to gain your vote.

The ban against certain countries flying their people in to America is for **Your protection, the protection of your family, as well as the future of our country.** There has been a huge influx of terrorist-associated countries flying unknowns into our Nation, which very well may be setting up more and more secret cells in your city! How easily you all have forgotten 9/11, the Boston Marathon, the Paris bombings, and so many other horrible acts by these extremists! But I guess if you didn't lose someone special in those tragedies, it may not matter to you that it can and will happen again! You all forget President Trump is only trying to protect you from the war against America that was declared by them many years ago; just remember you, your family, and friends all are AMERICANS! **So, no matter how much you protest and march on their behalf, they will still kill you and all that you love!** I'm not saying that all Muslims are bad, but we all need to Fight for what's Right: people, THE AMERICAN PEOPLE, and the American way of life that's being threatened! Your Activision and protests don't prove how caring and humane you are; it only shows how heartless, blind, and misguided you are to ignore the millions of family members in need in your own house while fighting so passionately for those non-family members from outside your house.

Give our American citizens who are HOMELESS a home, give our JOBLESS a job, feed our HUNGRY, march, and support the Native American people, Veterans, and Citizens of These United States of America!

Everyone from the homeless, refugees, or asylum seekers to the top politicians in this country should always put America First. If they can't or won't do that, they should leave immediately!

CHAPTER 12

THE U.S. CONSTITUTION

The U.S. Constitution is a lengthy document that outlines the framework of the government, including the preamble and seven articles. Here's a brief overview of its main components:

1. **Preamble**: Introduces the Constitution and states its purpose.
2. **Article I**: Establishes the Legislative Branch, detailing the powers and structure of Congress.
3. **Article II**: Outlines the Executive Branch, defining the powers of the President.
4. **Article III**: Creates the Judicial Branch, establishing the Supreme Court and other federal courts.
5. **Article IV**: Addresses the relationships between states and the federal government.
6. **Article V**: Describes the process for amending the Constitution.
7. **Article VI**: Establishes the Constitution as the supreme law of the land, along with the supremacy of federal laws.
8. **Article VII**: Outlines the process for ratification of the Constitution.

Additionally, there are 27 amendments, including the Bill of Rights (the first ten amendments), which guarantee individual liberties and rights.

The U.S. Constitution serves several key purposes that are foundational to the governance and structure of the United States.

1. **Framework for Government:** The Constitution establishes the structure of the federal government, outlining the powers and responsibilities of the three branches: the Legislative (Congress), the Executive (the President), and the Judicial (the Courts). This framework is designed to ensure a separation of powers and prevent any one branch from becoming too powerful.

2. **Rule of Law:** It enshrines the principle that the law applies equally to all individuals, including government officials. This helps to promote justice and maintain order in society.

3. **Protection of Rights:** The Constitution includes provisions that protect individual rights and liberties, particularly through the Bill of Rights, which consists of the first ten amendments. These amendments safeguard freedoms such as speech, religion, and assembly, as well as rights to due process and fair trial.

4. **Federalism:** The Constitution delineates the division of powers between the federal government and the states, establishing a federal system that allows for local governance while maintaining a strong national government.

5. **Amendability:** It provides a process for amendments, allowing the Constitution to adapt to changing societal needs and values over time. This flexibility ensures that the document remains relevant.

6. **Unity and Identity:** The Constitution serves as a unifying document for the diverse states and peoples of the United States, establishing a common identity and purpose while allowing for regional differences.

7. **Limitation of Government Power:** By clearly defining the powers granted to the government, the Constitution seeks to limit governmental authority and protect citizens from potential tyranny.

Overall, the U.S. Constitution is designed to create a balanced and effective government while protecting the rights of individuals and promoting the common good.

The Bill of Rights, comprising the first ten amendments to the U.S. Constitution, has a profound influence on modern legal interpretations and the American legal landscape. Here are several ways it shapes contemporary law:

1. **Foundation of Individual Rights**: The Bill of Rights establishes fundamental rights and liberties that serve as a benchmark for legal interpretations. Courts often reference these rights when determining cases related to freedom of speech, religion, assembly, and due process.

2. **Judicial Review**: The Bill of Rights empowers courts to review laws and government actions to ensure they do not infringe upon the rights guaranteed by these amendments. This judicial review has led to landmark decisions that shape public policy and societal norms.

3. **Incorporation Doctrine**: Through the doctrine of incorporation, many of the rights in the Bill of Rights have been applied to state governments via the Fourteenth Amendment. This has expanded the reach of individual rights beyond just the federal level, influencing state laws and practices.

4. **Legal Precedents**: Supreme Court decisions interpreting the Bill of Rights establish legal precedents that shape future cases. Landmark rulings, such as those on free speech (e.g., *New York Times Co. v. Sullivan*) or the right to bear arms (e.g., *District of Columbia v. Heller*), continue to inform legal arguments and decisions.

5. **Evolving Interpretations**: The Bill of Rights is subject to evolving interpretations as societal values change. Courts may reinterpret these amendments

to address contemporary issues, such as digital privacy rights and the implications of social media on free speech.

6. **Balancing Rights and Interests**: Legal interpretations often involve balancing individual rights against government interests or community safety. The Bill of Rights provides a framework for this balancing act, influencing how courts weigh competing interests.

7. **Public Discourse and Advocacy**: The Bill of Rights shapes public discourse about rights and liberties, influencing advocacy efforts and legislative initiatives. Movements for civil rights, privacy rights, and other social issues often invoke the protections of the Bill of Rights to support their causes.

Overall, the Bill of Rights remains a vital part of the American legal system, influencing not only court decisions but also the broader societal understanding of rights and liberties in a democratic society.

CHAPTER 13

A.C.L.E.

AMERICAN CITIZENS LAW ENFORCEMENT

Dedicated to the Enforcement of Ignored, Overlooked, and Misguided Federal, State, & Local Laws against Felonious Criminals, Illegal Immigrants, Corrupt Politicians and Terrorists both Domestic & Abroad.

What We Stand For, Against & the Laws We Will Enforce

- Against - The destruction of the American way of life, prosperity.
- For - Regeneration of American pride, prosperity and unity.
- Against - American Veterans being Homeless, Hungry & Jobless.
- For - Any tax money given to illegals, refugees etc. now goes to Homeless Vets.
- For - English as our (ONLY) National Language.
- Against - Government having ANY control over our personal/family lives.
- Against - Absolute Government Control - New World Order.
- Against - Gun Control, all American Citizens should be able to defend themselves.
- For - American Citizens vote every 4 years for every political office.
- Against - Constant Increase in Laws that affect Citizens and Not Politicians.
- For - Control over Politicians, finances, and their benefits while serving limited terms.
- Against - IRS - Internal Revenue Service, its absurd Enforcement Powers.
- Against - Constant Over Taxation with No Representation, Increased Taxes.
- For - A set 5% tax on everybody including Government employees/Politicians.
- Against - Open Borders.
- For - Intense Border Control and Enforcement / Closed Borders.
- Against - Illegal Immigration, Dream Act, and Sanctuary Cities.
- Against - Unlimited terms for Government Aid recipients.
- For - 6 months to 1 year at most For Aid, including Section 8.
- Against - More Aid for More Kids. Don't have kids if you can't support yourself.
- For - Immediate deportation of all Illegal Immigrants from whatever country.
- Against - Government Aid of Any Type for non-Citizens.
- Against - Foreign Aid of any and all kind including refugees.
- For - All Foreign Aid funds go to homeless American Citizens.
- Against - Excessive Licenses, Fees, Taxes, and miscellaneous charges.

- Against - Unproductive Members of Society as Career Benefits recipients.
- For - Putting every unemployed American to work. (Replacing Immigrants).
- Against - Forced Health Care (Obamacare) & being taxed if you can't afford it.
- For - Optional Health Care that is very affordable for American Citizens.
- Against - Non-specific gender identification / bathroom usage, etc.
- For - If you have male chromosomes, you're Male / female chromosomes, you're not.
- Against - Trying to introduce unqualified foreign nationalists into our Government.
- Against- People living America against our Country, our Flag, & our Values.
- For - Everyone against America & our way of life to go home where they belong.
- Against - American Government trying to Police the World and their issues.
- For - Immediate removal of any Politician that acts for themselves or large Corporations and not in the best interest of the American people.

CHAPTER 14

CENSORSHIP IN AMERICA

Definition: Censorship is the suppression or restriction of speech, public communication, or other information that may be considered objectionable, harmful, sensitive, or inconvenient by authorities, institutions, or other entities. This can include the removal, alteration, or prohibition of content in various forms, such as books, films, music, news articles, and online content. Censorship can be employed for various reasons, including political control, moral standards, national security, or social stability. It can be implemented by governments, organizations, or even individuals, and often raises debates concerning freedom of expression and the right to information.

The First Amendment to the United States Constitution protects several fundamental rights. It states:

"Congress shall make no law respecting an establishment of religion, or prohibiting the free exercise thereof, or abridging the *freedom of speech*, or of the press; or the right of the people peaceably to assemble, and to petition the Government for a redress of grievances."

In summary, it guarantees freedoms concerning what we say, religion, expression, assembly, and the right to petition the government.

This is exactly what's been happening since the top Social Platforms were lowered into the sewer with the corrupt U.S. Government. They have silenced our words, our videos, our movies and our posts. We have been stopped from expressing our thoughts and feelings, our opinions, likes and dislikes. Americans should be able to say whatever they want to say, yes, feelings may get hurt or someone may not like what is being said, but so what...Don't read it. Everyone should have the right to express their thoughts and feelings without being suppressed! The worst suppressors of the American voice have been this nasty group of corrupt and misguided platforms:

1. **Facebook / Instagram** - they created their "Independent Fact Checkers" / Facebook account suspensions, community standards, and or deactivations for anybody that spoke against or had a different opinion than the narrative being put out by the mainstream media and government.

2. **Twitter** - this crappy platform blocked and canceled accounts for people saying things that hurt Liberal feelings...luckily this company was bought out by Elon Musk and is now called X.

3. **YouTube** - A video platform where now your videos were being scrutinized and removed if you spoke or demonstrated the truth.

All of these platforms knew the truth about the government-run COVID-19 pandemic and its evil Vaccines that people were being forced to take, people were having complications from and people were dying from . Americans were silenced from speaking the truth about the origins of Covid, alternative medicine and even from saying the words "Covid" and or "Vaccines" in their posts/videos. They'd instantly get flagged, labeled as misinformation, warned, suspended, or even canceled just for mentioning them or going against the narrative being put out. This was just plain wrong!

Our concerns about censorship on social media platforms like Facebook, Twitter, YouTube, and Instagram have been a problem for years now, especially regarding sensitive subjects like the COVID-19 pandemic and vaccines. Many Americans express frustration over content moderation practices that they believe suppress free speech or limit access to information. The debate often centers around the balance between curbing misinformation and allowing free speech / open dialogue. This issue highlights the challenges that social media companies face in managing content while adhering to community standards, legal regulations, or the requests from a tyrannical government.

Excessive censorship can have a range of negative consequences for society, including:

1. **Suppression of Free Speech**: Censorship limits individuals' ability to express their thoughts and opinions, leading to a culture of fear where people may self-censor to avoid repercussions, which is what you see with the "PC" movement.

2. **Stifling of Creativity and Innovation**: When ideas are restricted, it can hinder artistic and intellectual endeavors, leading to a lack of diversity in creative expressions and innovations.

3. **Misinformation and Lack of Transparency**: Censorship can result in the spread of misinformation, as the public may not have access to accurate or complete information necessary for informed decision-making by oneself and not just what the government or corporations want you to hear.

4. **Erosion of Trust**: Excessive censorship can lead to distrust in institutions, as people may believe that information is being manipulated for political or ideological purposes by a corrupt and tyrannical government who only want their narrative heard.

5. **Social Division**: When certain viewpoints are censored, it can create polarization within society, as marginalized voices become more isolated and unable to contribute to public discourse.

6. **Violation of Human Rights**: Censorship often infringes on fundamental human rights, including the right to free expression, which can lead to broader human rights abuses.

7. **Chilling Effect**: The fear of censorship may deter individuals from engaging in discussions on important social, political, or cultural issues, limiting public debate and discourse.

8. **Cultural Homogeneity**: Censorship can lead to a lack of representation of diverse perspectives and cultures, resulting in a homogenized cultural landscape that does not reflect the richness of society.

Overall, excessive censorship can undermine democratic values, hinder social progress, and diminish the overall quality of public discourse.

*

Truth - *They want to silence us all and control the distribution of information.*

We Will Never Know the Truth Unless We See It, Live It Already Know It Ourselves

What a disgusting shame that even our Information Platforms that give available information and the supposed truth behind all the world's happenings are still being directed away from the truth and still support the evil agenda of the Globalist Elites.

I have attempted many times to research information for a better understanding of World Issues and people through Google "Siri" and "ChatOn AI" and have mostly received fraudulent, watered down half-truths or complete redirections on many subjects and from what I already knew was the truth.

Many times I already knew the truth, but when I ask, I am redirected to what it is that they want me to believe instead of just giving factual information. Unfortunately, you can't believe the News, Movies, or even the Internet Information Platforms! Sadly, We can't believe anything in this World, as it is all being entered by those who want to control the narrative and what information we read and believe.

The control of information is the management and regulation of information and knowledge dissemination. It encompasses various aspects, including censorship, data privacy, information security, and the influence of media. Governments, organizations, and individuals may control information for various reasons, such as controlling their tyrannical narratives and/or for shaping the public's perception.

Some Key factors in the control of information include:

1. **Censorship:** The suppression of speech, public communication, or other information from information platforms such as "Google," "Siri," and others that may be considered objectionable or harmful to their agenda.

2. **Data Privacy:** Regulations and practices that protect personal information from unauthorized access and misuse.

3. **Misinformation and Disinformation:** The spread of false information, either unintentionally (misinformation) or intentionally (disinformation), which can influence public opinion and behavior. These practices are being portrayed by information platforms such as Google, Siri, and ChatOn AI, along with many others that are controlled by liberal/corrupt activists.

4. **Media Control:** The ownership and influence of media outlets over the information that is disseminated to the public, which can affect public awareness and understanding of issues. These deceptive practices were done by the Biden Administration for 4 years.

5. **Digital Surveillance:** The monitoring of individuals' online activities by governments or corporations, impacting privacy and freedom of expression.

CHAPTER 15

AMERICAN TAX MONEY TO SUPPORT ILLEGAL ALIENS / REFUGEES / FOREIGNERS

The subject of American tax money being used to support illegal aliens, refugees, and foreigners is a complex and controversial issue. It often centers around debates on immigration policy, social services, and the allocation of government funds. This subject reverts back to the idea that American tax dollars shouldn't be for the Government to spend frivolously on whatever they choose and rather only for the benefit of the U.S. taxpayers.

Supporters of providing assistance argue that it is a humanitarian obligation to help those in need, particularly refugees fleeing violence and persecution. They may point to the economic contributions that immigrants make to society and the workforce. But as we know, there is violence in every nation, and most do not offer any economic contribution and just feed off of our systems.

Opponents often argue that taxpayer money should prioritize U.S. citizens and legal residents only, expressing concerns about the potential strain on public services and resources. American citizens must qualify for these services, so non-citizens shouldn't be able to come and receive them readily.

This topic brings up various aspects, including legal frameworks, ethical considerations, and the impact on communities.

If certain people wish to take the humanitarian route to aiding illegal aliens, refugees, or asylum seekers, then they should give their own money to a specific cause to serve that purpose. Most Americans are having a hard enough time working and supporting themselves and their own families. They shouldn't have to, nor do they want to support people who shouldn't even be in this country.

Our responsibility is to our country, ourselves, and our families; anything additional should be done on a voluntary basis. The government is stealing more of our money than they need and then just handing it out to these foreigners like it's an everlasting supply of water. If the government has so much money that they can support those non-citizens in our country, as well as the billions of dollars to foreign countries, then we are paying way too much in taxes!

Undocumented immigrants / Illegal Aliens in the United States may access several benefits and services, although their eligibility can be limited and varies by state. Some specific benefits include:

- **Cash Money -**
- **Free Hotel Rooms -**
- **Free Cellphones -**
- **Free Plane Fights -**
- **Drivers Licenses -**
- **Free Housing -**
- **Free Food -**

1. **Medical Care**: Many states provide free medical services to undocumented immigrants, particularly in life-threatening situations.

2. **Public Health Programs**: Some states offer public health services, including vaccinations and maternal and child health services, regardless of immigration status.

3. **Education**: Undocumented children have the right to attend public schools from kindergarten through 12th grade. Some states also allow undocumented students to access in-state tuition rates for college.

4. **Workplace Protections**: Undocumented immigrants are entitled to certain labor protections, including safe working conditions and the right to report wage theft.

5. **Food Assistance**: While most federal food assistance programs require proof of legal status, some states provide food aid to undocumented residents, particularly for children.

6. **Community Services**: Various nonprofit organizations and community groups offer support services, including legal aid, housing assistance, and counseling.

7. **Driver's Licenses**: Some states allow undocumented immigrants to obtain driver's licenses or permits, which can help them access employment and services.

8. **Legal Representation**: Organizations often provide free or low-cost legal assistance to help undocumented immigrants navigate immigration issues.

While these benefits are available for undocumented immigrants, many Americans that are "Legal Citizens" go homeless, hungry, and without proper medical care. They are lost and forgotten by our Government just so they can keep up the facade that this is a giving and caring country filled with opportunities.

Americans Don't Want to Support Illegal Immigrants

The fact that many Americans do not want to support illegal immigrants, refugees, or asylum seekers with tax dollars is a significant aspect of the immigration debate. We have our own families that we work to support and should have NO obligation to work our asses off and support anyone else's. Here are a few reasons to support this perspective:

1. **Economic Concerns**: Some people believe that providing assistance to undocumented immigrants or refugees may strain public resources and services, such as healthcare, education, and welfare systems. They argue that taxpayer money should only benefit American citizens.

2. **Security Issues**: There are concerns about national security and the potential for illegal immigration to pose risks. Some Americans feel that resources should be directed toward ensuring the safety and security of the nation from gangs, drug traffickers, human traffickers, domestic animal eaters, and other criminals.

3. **Legal and Fairness Issues**: Many believe that supporting individuals who have entered the country illegally undermines the rule of law and the efforts of those who follow legal immigration processes. What's the purpose of law if you don't follow the law and nobody is above the law?

4. **Cultural Integration**: There are worries about the integration of immigrants into American society. Some fear that providing support may lead to cultural tensions or challenges in assimilation.

5. **Political Rhetoric**: Political narratives often shape public opinion. Discussions around immigration can be polarizing, and political leaders may emphasize the costs associated with supporting immigrants to rally their base.

Plain and simple, the "Invasion" of foreign nationals / "Imported Political Army" into our country must stop immediately. They don't belong here, we don't want them here, and we absolutely don't want to support them in any way through our tax dollars, social services, or welfare programs. American tax dollars for America and Americans only!

Ways we can Slow or Stop illegal migration?

Addressing illegal migration is a multifaceted challenge that requires a combination of strategies. The number one thing is to be sure that no services or handouts are provided to any illegal alien. If we don't provide free services such as healthcare, etc., they'll have no reason to come here and drain our resources that are needed for Americans.

Here are some other potential options:

1. **Strengthening Border Security**: Enhancing physical barriers, surveillance technologies, and armed patrols with authorization to shoot can help prevent unauthorized crossings. This may include investing in personnel and technology at borders along with U.S. citizen support and patrols. Some countries will shoot or imprison illegal entrants, and that possibility is enough to prevent the risk of entering our country illegally.

2. **Comprehensive Immigration Reform**: Implementing policies that create clear pathways for legal immigration can reduce the incentive for individuals to migrate illegally. This could involve adjusting visa programs to meet labor market needs and harsh penalties for those who choose illegal crossing.

3. **Addressing Root Causes**: Many people migrate due to violence, poverty, and lack of opportunities in their home countries. Supporting development programs, conflict resolution, and economic assistance in their own countries can help address these underlying issues.

4. **International Cooperation**: Collaborating with other countries to manage migration flows can be effective. This includes sharing intelligence, coordinating border management, and establishing safe and legal migration channels. We shouldn't support countries that aren't taking care of their own problems and people. We have our own problems; stay home and fix yours while we're busy trying to fix ours!

5. **Enforcement of Immigration Laws**: Strengthening the enforcement of existing immigration laws can deter illegal migration. This includes pursuing employers who hire undocumented workers and ensuring harsh consequences for those who hire illegal workers or people who overstay visas.

6. **Public Awareness Campaigns**: Educating potential migrants about the risks and harsh penalties of illegal migration and the realities of life in another country can help reduce the number of individuals attempting to migrate illegally. Letting them know that coming into our country illegally will not give them any benefits of any type that are designed for American citizens.

7. **Asylum and Refugee Processes**: Streamlining and improving the efficiency of asylum and refugee processing can ensure that those fleeing persecution have a safe and legal way to seek refuge.

8. **Community Engagement**: Involving local communities in citizen patrols, having better awareness and knowledge of the dangers of invading migrants. Educate them on recognizing illegals, not hiring them, and possibly apprehending them for the immigration authorities to take.

So you have most Americans opposed to any illegal immigration and definitely against any of our money/services being spent on them, but if those who choose their so-called "humanitarian" side of the issue, then they should spend their own personal money supporting and housing these individuals/families until Immigration Services locates and deports them.

Each of these strategies has its own challenges and implications that can be worked out for the defense of our country.

WELFARE SHOULD BE EARNED BY CONTRIBUTING CITIZENS, NOT HANDED OUT TO THOSE WHO BREAK THE RULES.

CHAPTER 16

THEY'RE POISONING OUR FOOD

Proposition 65 WARNING

Chemicals Known To The State Of California To Cause Cancer or Birth Defects or Other Reproductive Harm Are Present In The Food or Beverages Sold Here. For Example, Many Grilled Foods, Such as Flame-Cooked Beef, Contain Polycyclic Aromatic Hydrocarbons (PAHs) Which Are Formed as A Byproduct Of Grilling.

It's said that the large food corporations are possibly in league with the medical/pharmaceutical corporations to help keep us sick and with symptoms/health issues. Collaboration between them for evil profits: Why else would natural/organic foods cost more than heavily processed, sugary junk foods? Why else would they be constantly working to develop artificial foods such as meats?

Why are they poisoning our water with fluoride and other products? They're poisoning our meat products by injecting the MRNA Vaccine in Beef, Chicken, and Pork products without our consent. Any and all side effects from these poisons will obviously be handled by the pharmaceutical companies that'll be right there, ready to get us all hooked up on their drugs.

You have to wonder how much of this is true when you have a tech billionaire buying up thousands of acres of food-growing land and spraying his new additives "aPEEL" on our foods. His Bill and Melinda Gates Foundation has already been kicked out of various countries such as India and is facing legal issues for poisoning children/people with their experimental vaccines.

Apeel's own <u>FDA documents</u> reveal that the manufacturing process involves toxic heavy metals and solvents, which can accumulate in the human body over time and contribute to numerous health conditions, including chronic illness.

Concerns about food safety and the presence of chemicals/pests, dyes, and other additives in food are quite significant. The American people are advocating for more transparency in food labeling and stricter regulations on food production to ensure that what food we consume is safe and healthy. Especially since most additives in American food are banned in other countries.

It's important to stay informed about what is in our food and support practices that promote natural and organic options whenever possible. Additionally, discussing these concerns with local representatives or participating in community awareness programs can help drive change in food safety standards.

They are now in 2025 planning to inject the MRNA Vaccine into our food animals so that they can (without our consent) get their poison into every U.S. Citizen who may eat beef, chicken, and or pork products! This is an assault against the American people; if a person were to secretly put anything into a food product, they'd be arrested and prosecuted for poisoning and assault. Why and How are these people getting away with this Crap!

<u>Here are some common food additives that people should be aware of:</u>

1. **Preservatives**: Chemicals like sodium benzoate and potassium sorbate are used to extend shelf life but can cause reactions in sensitive individuals.

2. **Artificial Sweeteners**: Substitutes like aspartame, Sucralose, and saccharin are often found in diet foods and drinks, but some studies suggest potential health risks.

3. **Coloring Agents**: Artificial dyes, such as Red 40 and Yellow 5, are used to enhance appearance but may cause allergic reactions in some people.

4. **Flavor Enhancers**: Monosodium glutamate (MSG) is used to enhance flavor but can lead to symptoms in those sensitive to it, often referred to as "Chinese restaurant syndrome."

5. **Emulsifiers**: Ingredients like carrageenan and lecithin are used to improve texture but can cause digestive issues for some.

6. **Trans Fats**: Partially hydrogenated oils are used for texture and shelf stability but are linked to heart disease and other health issues.

7. **Thickeners and Stabilizers**: Additives like xanthan gum or guar gum enhance texture but may affect digestion in some individuals.

8. **Flour Bleaching Agents**: Chemicals like benzoyl peroxide are used to whiten flour, but their long-term effects are debated.

9. **Seed Oils**: Industrial seed oils are highly processed oils extracted from the seeds of various plants like soybeans, corn, rapeseed (the source of canola oil), cottonseed, and safflower seeds.

Industrial seed oils are primarily polyunsaturated fats, which means that their chemical structure has many unsaturated or double bonds (poly = many). The reason this matters is that double bonds are a source of vulnerability in a fat. Eight of the concerning seed oils are Canola, Sunflower, Safflower, corn, Soybean, Cotton Seed, Grape-Seed and Rice Bran.

Seed oils weren't introduced into our food supply until the early 1900s. Interestingly, they got their start when businessmen Proctor & Gamble wanted to find a cheaper alternative to animal fats for their new bar of soap. They started mass producing cottonseed oil, a waste product of cotton farming and even created a subsidiary of their business to manage its production and operations.

Being aware of these additives can help you make more informed choices about the foods you consume. Reading labels and opting for whole, unprocessed foods can significantly reduce exposure to these substances.

The idea that the U.S. government and the FDA manipulate food to keep people unhealthy is allegedly a conspiracy theory, but with completely different ingredients in American food products compared to the same products in other countries, those conspiracies seem quite plausible.

The FDA's primary role is to ensure the safety and efficacy of food and pharmaceuticals. While there are legitimate concerns about food safety, labeling, and the financial influence of large food corporations, the assertion that there is a coordinated effort to keep people unhealthy is questionable.

Public health initiatives often aim to promote better nutrition and reduce diseases linked to poor diet. However, issues like food industry lobbying and the complexity of food systems can lead to debates about regulations and practices.

I've seen a bear not eat a supposed hamburger patty. I've seen cheese not melt. I've seen a torch that did not destroy a cookie, and I've seen birds not eat bread. If it's not scary to see animals recognize the dangers of "fake food," I don't know what is.

Several food additives are banned in Europe, but they are still permitted in the United States. Here are some of those additives that are banned due to negative health risks.

1. **Azodicarbonamide (ADA):** Often used as a dough conditioner in bread products, this additive is banned in Europe due to concerns about its potential health effects.

2. **Potassium Bromate:** This additive is used to strengthen dough in bread-making. It has been linked to cancer in animal studies and is banned in the EU, while still allowed in the U.S.

3. **Brominated Vegetable Oil (BVO):** Used to keep citrus-flavored soft drinks mixed, BVO is banned in Europe due to potential health risks but is still used in some American beverages.

4. **Artificial Food Colorings (certain types):** Some synthetic colorings, such as Yellow 5 and Red 40, are subject to stricter regulations in Europe, and certain variants are banned, while they are more commonly used in the U.S.

5. **Ractopamine:** A feed additive used to promote leanness in pigs and cattle, it is banned in the EU due to health concerns but is still permitted in the U.S.

6. **Certain Preservatives:** Some preservatives, like BHA and BHT, are allowed in the U.S. but face more stringent regulations in Europe due to potential health concerns.

7. **Sudan dyes**: Also known as azo dyes, these dyes are carcinogens that can cause genetic defects and skin allergies.

8. **Titanium dioxide (E171)**: The European Food Safety Authority (EFSA) concluded that titanium dioxide is no longer safe as a food additive.

9. **Artificial dyes**: Some dyes have been linked to attentional problems in children.

A Food System Dependent on Chemicals isn't a Food System; it's a Chemical System.

In the United States, several pesticides are commonly used on food crops, and they are produced by various companies. Unfortunately, many, if not all, of these pesticides are causing irreparable damage to the soil, the food, and to our citizens who eat it. Here are some notable pesticides along with their manufacturers:

1. **Glyphosate** - Manufactured by Monsanto (now part of Bayer), glyphosate is a widely used herbicide effective against a broad spectrum of weeds.

2. **Atrazine** - Produced by Syngenta, atrazine is a herbicide primarily used on corn and is known for its effectiveness in controlling weeds.

3. **Chlorpyrifos** - Originally made by Dow AgroSciences (now part of Corteva), chlorpyrifos is an insecticide used on various crops, though its use has been restricted in some states due to health concerns.

4. **Imidacloprid** - Developed by Bayer, this neonicotinoid insecticide is commonly used to control pests on a variety of crops.

5. **Carbaryl** - Manufactured by Bayer, carbaryl is an insecticide used on fruits, vegetables, and ornamentals.

6. **Paraquat** - Produced by Syngenta, paraquat is an herbicide used to control weeds and grasses, especially in cotton and soybean production.

7. **Dicamba** - Marketed by Bayer and BASF, dicamba is a herbicide used primarily on soybeans and cotton that are genetically modified to tolerate it.

These are just a few examples, and the use of pesticides can vary widely depending on the crop, region, and specific agricultural practices. They may help reduce or eliminate the pests, but they're also creating neurological damage to young children.

The use of pesticides in agriculture can have several potential environmental damaging impacts, including:

1. **Soil Health Degradation:** Pesticides can disrupt microbial communities in the soil, reducing biodiversity and impairing soil health. This can lead to decreased soil fertility and increased erosion.

2. **Water Contamination:** Pesticides can leach into groundwater or run off into surface water bodies, contaminating drinking water sources and harming aquatic ecosystems. This can affect fish and other wildlife.

3. **Non-target Species Impact:** Pesticides can harm non-target organisms, including beneficial insects (like pollinators), birds, and other wildlife. This can disrupt food webs and reduce biodiversity.

4. **Resistance Development:** Overuse of certain pesticides can lead to the development of resistance in pest populations, making them harder to control and leading to increased pesticide use.

5. **Air Pollution:** Some pesticides can volatilize and become airborne, contributing to air pollution and potentially impacting human health and the environment.

6. **Ecosystem Imbalance:** Pesticide use can alter the balance of ecosystems, leading to pest outbreaks or infestations of secondary pests due to the removal of their natural predators.

7. **Long-term Residual Effects:** Certain pesticides can persist in the environment for long periods, leading to long-term ecological impacts and potential bioaccumulation in food chains.

8. **Impact on Human Health:** While not strictly an environmental impact, pesticide runoff and exposure can affect human health, particularly for communities near agricultural areas.

Overall, while pesticides can be effective in managing pests and increasing agricultural productivity, their environmental impacts highlight the need for integrated pest management practices and sustainable agricultural methods that aren't harmful to the environment or humans in any way.

Pesticides and chemicals sprayed on foods can have several damaging/negative effects on human health, including:

1. **Acute Poisoning:** Exposure to high levels of pesticides can lead to immediate health issues such as nausea, vomiting, headaches, dizziness, and respiratory distress. In severe cases, it can result in hospitalization or even death.

2. **Chronic Health Effects:** Long-term exposure to certain pesticides has been linked to chronic health conditions, including:
   - **Cancer:** Some pesticides are classified as carcinogenic and have been linked to various types of cancer, including lymphoma and leukemia.
   - **Endocrine Disruption:** Pesticides can interfere with hormonal systems, potentially leading to reproductive issues, developmental problems, and hormonal imbalances.

3. **Neurological Effects:** Some pesticides, particularly organophosphates and carbamates, can affect the nervous system, leading to cognitive impairments, memory issues, and other neurological disorders.

4. **Respiratory Problems:** Inhalation of pesticide residues can exacerbate respiratory conditions such as asthma or lead to new respiratory issues.

5. **Reproductive Health Issues:** Pesticide exposure has been associated with fertility problems, birth defects, and developmental disorders in children.

6. **Immune System Suppression:** Some studies suggest that exposure to pesticides may weaken the immune system, making individuals more susceptible to infections and diseases.

7. **Digestive Issues:** Pesticide residues on food can disrupt gut microbiota and contribute to digestive problems.

8. **Bioaccumulation:** Certain pesticides can accumulate in human tissues over time, leading to increased health risks as exposure continues.

The health effects of pesticides can vary based on the type of pesticide, the level and duration of exposure, individual susceptibility, and other factors.

Bill Gates - Apeel Technology Inc.

It is said to "extend the shelf-life of crops without refrigeration and protect them from being eaten by pests by developing a molecular camouflage that uses cutin from plant extracts to create an edible, ultrathin barrier on the crop surfaces."

aPeel technology, which involves applying a natural protective layer made from plant materials to fruits and vegetables, has garnered various opinions.

Positive Aspects:

1. **Extended Shelf Life:** Many support aPeel for its ability to significantly prolong the freshness of produce, reducing food waste.

2. **Natural Ingredients:** It uses edible, plant-based materials, which appeals to consumers looking for natural solutions.

3. **Sustainability:** Proponents argue that aPeel aligns with sustainable practices by minimizing the need for plastic packaging and reducing spoilage.

Concerns:

1. **Consumer Awareness:** Some people are unaware of what aPeel is, leading to skepticism about its safety and effectiveness.

2. **Labeling Issues:** There are calls for clear labeling to ensure consumers know when aPeel technology is used, as transparency is crucial.

3. **Perception of Freshness:** Some consumers might perceive treated produce as less fresh or natural compared to untreated options.

While aPeel technology is supposedly designed to be safe and is said to use edible, plant-based materials, there are only some of the listed health risks and concerns that consumers may think about:

PFIZER JUST RELEASED IT'S LIST OF SIDE EFFECTS OF ITS "COVID-19 VACCINE" ....and the list of some side effects of the Pfizer-Biontech Covid-19 Vaccine. TAKE-HEED!

Blood thrombosis.
Acute kidney injury,
Acute flaccid myelitis,
Positive antisperm antibodies,
Brainstem embolism,
Brainstem thrombosis,
Cardiac arrest (hundreds of cases),
Heart failure,
Cardiac ventricular thrombosis,
Cardiogenic shock,
Central nervous system vasculitis,
Neonatal death,
Deep vein thrombosis,
Brainstem encephalitis,
Hemorrhagic encephalitis,
Frontal lobe epilepsy,
Foaming at the mouth,
Epileptic psychosis,
Facial paralysis,
Fetal distress syndrome,
Gastrointestinal amyloidosis,
Generalized tonic-clonic seizure,
Hashimoto's encephalopathy,
Hepatic vascular thrombosis,
Herpes zoster reactivation,
Hepatitis Immune-mediated,
Interstitial lung disease,
Jugular vein embolism,
Juvenile myoclonic epilepsy,
Liver damage,
Low birth weight,
Multisystem inflammatory syndrome in children,
Myocarditis,
Neonatal seizure,
Pancreatitis,
Pneumonia,
Stillbirth,
Tachycardia,
Temporal lobe epilepsy,
Testicular autoimmunity,
Thrombotic stroke,
Type 1 diabetes mellitus,
Neonatal venous thrombosis,
Vertebral artery thrombosis,
Pericarditis,
Sudden death."

We just thought you'd like to know, because one thing people will never be able to say is, "I didn't know" WE TOLD YA!!

1. **Allergic Reactions:** Some individuals may have allergies or sensitivities to specific plant ingredients used in the aPeel coating, which could lead to allergic reactions when consumed.

2. **Chemical Residues:** Although aPeel is marketed as a natural solution, there may still be concerns about any chemical residues that could remain on the surface of the produce, especially if the coating is not properly regulated or monitored.

3. **Digestive Issues:** For some people, consuming unfamiliar substances, even if natural, could lead to digestive discomfort or other gastrointestinal issues.

4. **Nutrient Absorption:** There are concerns that coatings, in some cases, might impede the absorption of nutrients or alter the bioavailability of certain vitamins and minerals in the produce.

5. **Misleading Safety Perceptions**: The presence of a protective coating might lead consumers to overlook proper washing or handling practices, potentially increasing the risk of foodborne illnesses.

6. **Long-Term Effects:** Since aPeel technology is relatively new, the long-term health effects of consuming coated produce are not yet fully understood.

The FDA - Money Puppets
Food and Drug Administration

The Food and Drug Administration (FDA) is the regulatory agency of the United States Department of Health and Human Services. Its primary purpose is supposed to protect public health by ensuring the safety, efficacy, and security of various products. Unfortunately, just like so many other government-run agencies, they've become another puppet program that is corrupted by money and directed by those with nefarious agendas.

They allow poisons and harmful ingredients in American foods that are literally banned in many foreign countries. Our food production companies are allowed to include many additional additives into our foods that are addictive, poisonous, and outright harmful to our bodies, and it's all for "PROFIT."

The FDA's responsibilities are supposed to include:

1. **Food Safety:** Regulating food products to ensure they are safe for consumption and properly labeled. (Not Doing this Job - Gross Negligence).

2. **Drug Approval:** Overseeing the approval of pharmaceuticals and biological products to ensure they are safe and effective before they can be marketed. (Not doing this job - Gross Negligence).

3. **Medical Devices:** Regulating medical devices, including everything from simple items like band-aids to complex technologies like pacemakers.

4. **Cosmetics:** Ensuring that cosmetics are safe for use and labeled correctly.

5. **Tobacco Products:** Regulating the manufacturing, distribution, and marketing of tobacco products to protect public health.

6. **Public Health Initiatives:** Promoting public health initiatives and educating the public about health-related issues. (Counter-Acting against this initiative by allowing harmful additives to our food and passing harmful medications on to the market.)

Overall, the FDA plays a crucial role in ensuring that products consumed by the public are safe and meet established health standards. Their job is literally to protect us, but sadly, I truly believe that their Mission has fallen wayside for the benefit and profits of many companies and others.

TIPS and (BAD) SERVICE

The "tipping culture" has gotten so far out of hand that it's ridiculous. Back in the day, people chose the service profession as a job for which they were paid a specific amount for doing specific duties, just like any other job. With this job came the opportunity to receive (at the customers' discretion) an additional tip for exceptional service. As we know, not all servers have a great attitude or work ethic, and that's what encourages a customer to want to leave a tip.

Somehow, as time went on, tips were more expected regardless of their service, and for most of the time, the size of the tip would be based on your service. Doing this would do one of two things: 1. Let them know how well and appreciated their good service was, or 2. Let them know that their lack of service needs some attention and improvement. Again, as time went on, a specific amount of tips was now suggested and expected on receipts.

CHAPTER 17

GOVERNMENT COVERT TESTS ON AMERICANS

PsyOps - The art of mental, emotional, and physical disruption. Black-Ops

Your U.S. Government's covert operations and psychological operations (psyops) have a long history against their own American people, especially during times of conflict or social upheaval. These operations continue to this very day, proving that we are at constant war with our own government. They use movies, music, the news, television shows, social media, and other ways to spread propaganda to the citizens of this country and the world. Here are a few notable examples:

1. **MK-Ultra**: This was a CIA program that began in the 1950s, aimed at developing methods of mind control. It involved experiments on unwitting subjects, often using drugs like LSD, to assess their effects on behavior and cognition. The program raised significant ethical concerns and has been widely criticized, and yet it continues to operate covertly using many other modern-day chemicals and techniques. Many say this program is still going On today.

2. **Operation Northwoods**: Proposed in the early 1960s, this plan involved staging false-flag terrorist attacks to justify military intervention in Cuba. The plan was ultimately rejected by the Kennedy administration, but it highlights the lengths to which some government agencies may go to achieve political objectives. The same type of operation was used on 9/11 when the U.S. Government organized a fake terrorist attack that killed over 3000 Americans, saw the destruction of the New York skyscrapers (Twin Towers), and damage to the Pentagon to achieve political objectives.

3. **COINTELPRO**: The FBI's Counter Intelligence Program targeted civil rights organizations, feminist groups, and other activist movements from the 1950s to the 1970s. Tactics included infiltration, disinformation, and efforts to sow discord within groups, aiming to undermine their effectiveness and discredit their leaders. The government now uses the mainstream media and social media platforms to spread disinformation/misinformation to drive the world towards their narrative/agenda.

4. **Operation CHAOS**: This was a covert CIA initiative that aimed to monitor and infiltrate anti-war and civil rights groups in the 1960s and 70s. The operation collected intelligence on American citizens and sought to disrupt movements opposing government policies.

5. **Psy-Ops** during the Vietnam War: The U.S. military employed psychological operations to demoralize enemy troops and influence public opinion. This included broadcasting propaganda and using leaflets to spread disinformation about the war.

These operations often raise crucial ethical and legal questions regarding government transparency, citizen rights, and the balance of power. They illustrate the complex and sometimes troubling relationship between state security and individual freedoms. The government shouldn't be attacking their own people and using them like Guinea pigs; that's not national security.

Perceptions of government surveillance vary widely across cultures and can be influenced by historical context, political systems, societal norms, and individual experiences. Here are some general observations:

1. **Authoritarian Regimes**: In countries with authoritarian governments, surveillance is often viewed as a tool of oppression. Citizens may feel a heightened sense of fear and mistrust towards the state, leading to self-censorship and the suppression of dissent. Examples are North Korea and China, where extensive monitoring is commonplace.

2. **Democratic Societies**: In more democratic contexts, perceptions of surveillance can be mixed. Some citizens may view it as a necessary means of ensuring security and public safety, especially in the wake of terrorist threats. Others may express concern over privacy violations and the potential for abuse of power. Countries like the United States and many European nations often engage in public debates about the balance between security and civil liberties.

3. **Cultural Attitudes Toward Privacy**: In cultures that highly value individual privacy, such as many Western countries, there can be significant pushback against government surveillance. Citizens may advocate for stronger privacy protections and transparency. In contrast, cultures that prioritize communal safety and security may be more accepting of surveillance measures.

4. **Historical Context**: Historical experiences with government surveillance can shape current perceptions. For instance, countries with a history of state-sponsored surveillance and repression may have a more skeptical view of government intentions. For example, citizens in Eastern European countries might have lingering distrust due to past surveillance by communist regimes.

5. **Technology and Youth Culture**: Younger generations, who often grow up with technology and social media, may have a different relationship with surveillance. Some may accept surveillance as an inherent aspect of modern life, while others may be concerned about data privacy and the implications of constant monitoring.

6. **Globalization and Cross-Cultural Comparisons**: As globalization increases, cross-cultural perceptions of surveillance can influence one another. Exposure to different governmental practices and privacy norms can lead to shifts in attitudes as people compare their own experiences with those in other countries. The U.S. and other so-called "Elites" seem to be working towards their "New World Order" scam, which will put everyone in the world under surveillance and their control.

Overall, cultural perceptions of government surveillance are complex and multifaceted, often reflecting a blend of historical experiences, societal values, and individual beliefs.

Government testing on citizens, often referred to as unethical experimentation or human experimentation, has occurred throughout history, sometimes leading to significant controversies and public outcry. Here are some notable examples:

1. **Tuskegee Syphilis Study**: Conducted by the U.S. Public Health Service from 1932 to 1972, this study involved African-American men with syphilis who were misled into believing they were receiving treatment. Instead, they were left untreated to observe the natural progression of the disease, leading to severe health consequences and deaths.

2. **Project MK-Ultra**: As previously mentioned, this CIA program aimed to develop mind control techniques during the Cold War. It involved administering drugs, such as LSD, to unwitting subjects and conducting psychological experiments without their consent.

3. **The Stanford Prison Experiment**: While not a government initiative, this psychological study conducted by psychologist Philip Zimbardo in 1971 used college students to simulate a prison environment. The experiment quickly spiraled out of control, leading to psychological distress among participants prompting ethical discussions about human experimentation.

4. **Operation Sea-Spray**: In 1950, the U.S. Navy sprayed a bacterial agent over San Francisco to study the effects of biological warfare. The operation was conducted without the knowledge of the residents, leading to health concerns and ethical questions about consent and transparency.

5. **The Guatemala Syphilis Experiment**: In the 1940s, U.S. researchers conducted experiments on Guatemalan prisoners, soldiers, and psychiatric patients without their consent. They deliberately infected subjects with syphilis and other sexually transmitted diseases to test the effectiveness of penicillin.

6. **Radiation Experiments**: During the Cold War, the U.S. government conducted various experiments involving radiation exposure on unsuspecting citizens, including military personnel and hospital patients, to study the effects of radiation on human health.

7. **Vaccine Trials**: In some cases, vaccine trials have been conducted in vulnerable populations without adequate informed consent or ethical oversight. This raises important questions about the balance between public health benefits and individual rights. A recent example is the COVID-19 vaccine, where the U.S. government spread the Coronavirus throughout the U.S. and the world and then forced many people through threats and fear to take multiple doses due to fake variants/strains of the virus. Many people have new health issues that weren't there before, and others have died as a consequence of taking this so-called government medicine.

8. **Chem-Trails:** "Chemical Trails" is a theory that claims the visible trails left by aircraft in the sky are not simply contrails (condensation trails) formed by water vapor but are instead chemical or biological agents deliberately sprayed for various undisclosed purposes. More stories of these possibilities are coming to light by whistleblowers. Here are some key points related to these theories.

1. **Contrails vs. Chem trails:** Contrails are formed when water vapor from aircraft engines condenses and freezes in the cold upper atmosphere, creating visible clouds that disappear shortly thereafter...Chemtrail theorists argue that these trails last longer and spread out, leading to cloud-like formations that are not typical of regular contrails that dissipate.

2. **Alleged Purposes:** Proponents of the chem trail theory suggest various motives for the alleged spraying, including weather modification, population control, or the dispersal of harmful chemicals for nefarious purposes. Some also believe it is related to geoengineering efforts aimed at combating climate change.

3. **Public Health Concerns:** Some chem trail whistleblowers claim that the substances being sprayed are harmful to human health, contributing to respiratory issues and other health problems.

4. **Government Conspiracy:** The theory often involves claims that governments and secret organizations are involved in a cover-up, aiming to deceive the public about the true nature of these chemtrails and the harm that they can bring to humans.

5. **Cultural Impact:** The chem trail conspiracy theory has gained a significant following and has been discussed in various media outlets, documentaries, and social media platforms, contributing to public distrust in government and scientific institutions.

These instances highlight the importance of ethical standards, informed consent, and oversight in research involving human subjects. They have led to the establishment of stricter regulations and guidelines to protect individuals from exploitation in scientific and medical research. Through these experiments and unwilling trials, many have died or had their health compromised. Your own government is hurting or killing you, and it's not even for your benefit in any way.

They're Listening to Us

So, the U.S. Government used "False Flag" events to further their Tyrannical control over the people of the United States and even the world (as their lies would tie into the allies that believed what the government had said), such as 9/11. They planned and killed over 3000 of their own citizens to tighten the noose around the necks of Americans and gain more control over them by using "Fear" and the idea of safety/security as their tools.

The Government had the world believing that we were attacked by foreign nations and even set up fake reports and media stories to convince the people of this nation of the danger. They used this horrific event as a catalyst to put forth "The Patriot Act."

The USA PATRIOT Act, enacted in October 2001 in response to the September 11 terrorist attacks, supposedly aimed to enhance law enforcement's ability to prevent terrorism. The acronym stands for "Uniting and Strengthening America by Providing Appropriate Tools Required to Intercept and Obstruct Terrorism." We know now that this was not entirely true, it is used to infringe on the privacy, security, and lives of the American people.

Key provisions of the Act include:

1. **Increased Surveillance Powers:** Law enforcement agencies were granted expanded authority to conduct surveillance, including wiretaps and monitoring of internet communications.

2. **Information Sharing:** The Act facilitated greater information sharing among government agencies, allowing for improved coordination in counter-terrorism efforts.

3. **Financial Monitoring:** It included measures to track financial transactions and prevent money laundering, particularly in relation to funding terrorism.

4. **Detention and Deportation:** The law allowed for the detention of immigrants suspected of terrorism-related activities and streamlined the process for deportation.

5. **Roving Wiretaps:** Law enforcement could obtain wiretap orders that apply to any phone used by a suspect rather than being limited to a specific device.

The Patriot Act has been controversial, with critics arguing it infringes on civil liberties and privacy rights. Various provisions have been subject to legal challenges and legislative review over the years, resulting in modifications and renewals of certain aspects of the Act.

Through this, it's said that they listen through our phones, our televisions, our computers and iPads etc.

CHAPTER 18

GROWING UP WITH LIES AND FALSE FLAG ATTACKS

It's a sad world that we live in when almost everything that we were taught and learned as we were growing up has been a lie. Things that we're taught growing up, things that we're taught in school, and things that we're taught or told as we grow in life. The News Media actually has the right (from the Government) to lie and or misinform you. How sick is that? They guided us toward the beliefs of their narratives and commercial goals rather than in the reality of life.

We're led to believe only what they want us to believe.

If you're not aware, no homeowner even owns their home that they've paid for for 30 years! You must have a job that you're taxed from; you pay for the house that they tax you for, you're taxed for everything you buy for or do to your home, you pay for utilities and the government taxes you for, and yet after 30 years of payments, they still charge you "Property Taxes." Nobody owns their home, Government owns it, and you're just a renter!

Here, I'm touching on several historical narratives that have been re-examined and challenged over time. Many events in history, like Columbus's arrival in America, the origins of Thanksgiving, and even the moon landing, have complex and often controversial histories.

<u>False Flag Attacks</u>

A False Flag attack refers to covert operations designed to deceive by making it appear as though they are carried out by a different entity than the actual perpetrator. The term originates from naval warfare, where ships would fly flags of nations other than their own to deceive opponents. In contemporary contexts, False Flag attacks are often used in political or military strategies to manipulate public perception, justify military actions, or discredit opponents. These actions can involve staged events that are blamed on a specific group or country, creating a narrative that serves the interests of the attackers.

<u>**Here are several notable historical examples of False Flag operations:**</u>

1. **The Gleiwitz Incident (1939):** This operation was staged by Nazi Germany to justify the invasion of Poland. German operatives dressed as Polish soldiers attacked a German radio station and left behind dead bodies of concentration camp prisoners to make it appear as if Poland had launched an attack.

2. **Operation Northwoods (1962):** Proposed by the U.S. Department of Defense, this plan suggested staging terrorist attacks against American citizens and blaming them on Cuba to justify military intervention. Although it was never executed, it illustrates the concept of False Flag operations at a state level.

3. **The Reichstag Fire (1933):** The German parliament building was set on fire, and the Nazis blamed communist agitators. This event was used to consolidate power and suppress political opposition, raising suspicions that the Nazis may have been involved in the arson themselves.

4. **Operation Gladio (Cold War):** This was a NATO operation involving clandestine "stay-behind" armies in Europe. Some of these groups were implicated in terrorist attacks, which were then attributed to leftist organizations, creating a climate of fear and justifying anti-communist measures.

5. **The USS Maine Explosion (1898):** The sinking of the USS Maine in Havana Harbor was blamed on Spain, leading to the Spanish-American War. While the cause remains debated, some believe it may have been an accident, and the incident was used to rally public support for war.

These examples illustrate how False Flag operations can be used to manipulate public opinion and achieve political or military objectives, just like the Weapons of Mass Destruction in Iraq, Possibly the Titanic, the assassination of JFK, Possibly the Challenger Shuttle Disaster, 9/11, COVID-19 Pandemic and many more lies from our evil and deceitful government.

False Flag operations highlight the complex interplay of deception in international relations. They raise ethical questions about the lengths to which governments will go to achieve their objectives. Such operations can lead to:

* Loss of Trust: When the truth behind such operations is revealed, it can lead to public distrust in government institutions and media.

* Escalation of Conflicts: False Flag operations can escalate tensions and lead to wars based on fabricated narratives.

* Misinformation: They illustrate the power of misinformation in shaping public opinion and policy decisions.

Overall, False Flag operations serve as a reminder of the potential for manipulation and the importance of critical thinking in assessing world events.

1. **Columbus and America**: Columbus is often credited with "discovering" America, but this overlooks the fact that Indigenous peoples had been living on the entire continent for thousands of years. Past and recent finds have found other settlements that were here prior to Columbus, such as the Vikings (Leif Eriksson), who had visited North America centuries earlier. After a two-month ocean voyage, Columbus missed the mainland of the Americas and landed in the Bahamas on an island called San Salvador (formerly known as Guanahani) on October 12, 1492. It is also said that 13,000 - 13,500 years ago, the first known North Americans were known as "Clovis People," who arrived via a land bridge from Asia and Siberia. In 2015, new evidence suggests that Chinese explorers landed in the New World around 2500 years before Christopher Columbus.

2. **Thanksgiving**: The traditional story of Thanksgiving is often sanitized, omitting the harsh realities of colonization and the impact on Native American communities. In the Fall of 1621, the 'First" Thanksgiving took place as the Wampanoag people and the English Pilgrims celebrated a successful harvest in what is now called Plymouth, Massachusetts. It was in 1863 that President Abraham Lincoln made Thanksgiving an official holiday to improve relations between Northern and Southern States as well as between the U.S. and Tribal Nations.

The reality of Thanksgiving blends facts and myths of the time together and disregards the centuries of brutality against the Native Americans. Prior to the Pilgrims' arrival, Indigenous people did not experience illness, disease, overcrowding, or poor hygiene. Since the Europeans didn't bathe or change clothes much, they smelled bad to the Natives, who attempted to teach them to bathe but were unsuccessful. New England's Indigenous experienced a devastating death rate, with some tribes losing nearly every tribal member to the effects of the European diseases.

For Native Americans, Thanksgiving is a time for grief for all those ancestors who lost their lives and suffered after the arrival of European settlers. This is a National "Day of Mourning". One Native (Wamsutta James) wrote, "We, the Wampanoag, welcomed you, the white man, with open arms, little knowing that it was the beginning of the end."

3. **Christmas**: The date and many customs associated with Christmas have evolved over centuries, incorporating various cultural and religious traditions, such as the birth date of Jesus Christ. Before Christianity, Pagans celebrated the winter solstice at the end of December to mark the longer days and more sun. The Roman Emperor Constantine and The Catholic Church in Rome began celebrating Christmas on December 25the, 336 CE, to replace pagan celebrations. The church chose that date because it coincided with the winter solstice, which would attract non-Christian followers. The Bible doesn't specify the exact date of Jesus' birth, so the church declared December 25th the official Christmas holiday.

Some Puritans objected to the Christmas celebration because there is no mention in the Bible of the specific date of Jesus' birth date. They felt that the Christmas holiday was drunk and out of control. The Presbyterians in Scotland outlawed Christmas in 1640.

4. **JFK Assassination**: The assassination of President Kennedy has spawned numerous conspiracy theories, leading many to question the official account of events. It's suggested that the CIA had something to do with it; the global Elites had him killed because he wouldn't go along with their narrative, and others say it was the mob or the Cuba dictatorship that killed him.

Today, it's being said that it was various U.S. Government entities along with the Israeli Mossad that had him killed, and the kill shot was actually made by the driver of his caravan, who used his left hand over his right shoulder and fired the bullet that struck JKF in the head not long after the some Secret Service Agents who were supposed to run alongside the motorcade were mysteriously called off their posts.

Why was JFK killed? It's said that JFK would not go along with a wide variety of Global Elitists and their "False Flag Events," such as (Operation Northwood) where they wanted to shoot down a plane or blow up a US Ship, along with many other terrorist attacks against Americans so that they could then blame on Cuba to set up a full-scale invasion.

An article came out today, January 13, 2025, that stated that there is proof that Lyndon B Johnson and Richard Nixon both worked with the CIA in a covert operation to assassinate former President John F. Kennedy. Part of the deal was that LBJ would finish the term of President but not run for a second term, and Nixon would be allowed to run and win the presidency. Even at that time, the Director of the FBI (J. Edgar Hoover) stated, "The thing I am concerned about is having something issued so we can convince the public that Oswald is the real assassin, the only assassin." During that time, Jack Ruby also happened to be on Richard Nixon's payroll as an informant.

Strangely enough, the man with the most complete video footage of the assassination, Abraham Zapruder, was of Jewish Ukrainian decent, a 33-degree Freemason Inspector General Scottish Rite who was supposedly persuaded to take his camera to work that day. Within 24 hours of the assassination, he had a deal with Life Magazine for the footage; his heirs were later paid 16 million dollars; Earl Warren of the Warren Report) was also a 33-degree Freemason; every other person who filmed the assassination gave their footage over to the FBI and CIA,

As of January 20, 2025, President Donald J. Trump is the man who will finally declassify the JFK assassination files, and hopefully, the truth will finally be exposed.

March 18, 2025 - So 80,000 supposedly unredacted pages of the JFK report finally came out today, and just as many of us thought, the truth still will never be told. There was a lot more insight into American operations during that time and, of course, what happened after the President was shot, but as far as for what we were actually looking for (The Assassination), they just gave us what they wanted us to believe...SAME SHIT - "Lee Harvey Oswald Did It and Acted Alone!"

Unfortunately, over the last decade, we've found out that many Americans are gullible and brainless sheep, but there is so much obvious evidence against their bullshit narrative that sensible people will never believe their lies! I get it; if the "TRUTH" came out, The repercussions could be devastating to the Government, the CIA, The Israeli Mossad, and many more who may have had a hand in assassinating a sitting American President, so there was NO WAY that they'd actually let us know the 'TRUTH"!

5. **Moon Landing**: While the moon landing in 1969 is widely accepted, conspiracy theories suggest it was staged, reflecting broader distrust in government narratives. Multiple videos of green screen scenes have been brought into question as to whether or not the moon landing and many of the space projects were faked to look as though we beat the Russians to the moon.

6. **Seal Team Six**: The operation that killed Osama Bin Laden raised questions about transparency and the narratives surrounding national security.

Sources say that he (Bin Laden) wasn't really killed, and that is why Obama claimed to have immediately taken control of the body and then discarded it into the sea as if performing some sort of Muslim ritual. The story goes that Iran actually has or had control over the real Bin Laden and that the U.S. Government had to pay Iran $152,000,000,000 in cash to keep this information secret. From that point, Seal Team Six were the only loose ends, and that's why they were possibly shot down in the final mission of the helicopter (call sign - Extortion 17).

Seal Team Six used to carry out some of the military's riskiest missions, the ones considered too dangerous for conventional troops. They are a CTU (counter-terrorist unit) tasked with intelligence, counter-intelligence, investigations, and national security work.

7. **U.S. Establishment**: The founding of the United States involved complex motives, including colonial interests, various ideologies, and the impact of slavery, which are often simplified in traditional narratives.

8. **Halloween**: Often seen as a purely commercial holiday, Halloween has roots in the ancient Celtic festival of Samhain, which marked the end of the harvest season and was believed to be a time when the boundary between the living and the dead was blurred.

9. **Valentine's Day:** Commonly viewed as a day for romantic love, its origins can be traced back to the Roman festival of Lupercalia, which involved more pagan rituals celebrating fertility and matchmaking.

10. **Easter:** While many associate Easter with the resurrection of Jesus, the holiday also has origins in pagan spring festivals celebrating fertility and renewal, reflected in symbols like eggs and rabbits.

11. **September 11, 2001 (9/11):** The government would have you believe that a group (19) of unskilled Muslim terrorists in a very coordinated effort boarded (without being seen on cameras with their passports that they'd never need again on a "Domestic" flight) and hijacked 4 U.S. planes and strategically flew 2 of those planes into the "Twin Towers," (supposedly) 1 into the Pentagon (even though no plane was seen hitting the building nor was there parts to match the plain that they said hit the building) at an unprecedented 500+ miles per hour and the 4th (supposedly) crashed in an open area in Shanksville, Pennsylvania.

However, an overwhelming amount of evidence (by real non-government professionals/experts) against their lies has come forward, and it is now clearly obvious that the US Government, along with possibly the Israeli Mossad and others (Saudi Arabia), had a dirty hand in this American mass murder plot to steal more of our freedom away and drive this country and the world into war and their narratives.

It's strange that these agents of the government (so-called terrorists) got on to a one-way domestic flight with their passports and flew into a building that disintegrated them, the plane, and almost everything else, and yet somehow their passports were able to survive that and land (perfectly readable) on the ground below for the FBI to retrieve.

It's strange that just 6 weeks before 9/11, Larry Silverstein, who developed and owned building #7, then put only $15,000,000 (which he leveraged into 3.2 Billion dollars in the deal) of his own money in and acquired all the rest of the World Trade Center Buildings and took out a "Huge" insurance policy on them which included "Terrorist Attacks."

Silverstein had breakfast near the top of one of the Twin Towers every morning, but on September 11th, he just so happened to have an early and unexpected doctor's appointment. He mentioned in an interview that he and the firefighter made the decision to "Pull the Building".... The firefighters were told NOT to fight the fire and that the building had structural damage. Experts say it is quite obvious that "Building #7 was definitely a controlled demolition.

It's plain and simple that this was an inside job, a flat-out Conspiracy. So many experts, as well as audio/video proof, clearly demonstrate this. People said that weeks before the tragedy, strange trucks went into the buildings during times when nobody else was supposed to be there. You can see explosions from right before the planes hit the building; you can see explosions in various places in the building. Survivors in the building said that they saw, heard, or felt the explosions. The buildings wouldn't have pulverized the steel and concrete from fire. Fifteen floors of damaged building wouldn't take down 90 floors of 90,000 tons of structural steel that's below it.

All the evidence points to a huge and disgusting government conspiracy against its own people that clearly says, "Treason!" None of their so-called "Official Version" of the story makes any sense, especially when the Twin Towers were specifically designed and built to withstand being struck by huge airplanes. Flight 93 (a Boeing 757 - 100-ton airplane) supposedly crashed, and yet there were no actual plane pieces that could be recognized as a plane in the burnt hole in the ground. Not the local news media, local townspeople, nor the local mayor believed that a plane actually crashed in their town of Shanksville. People also would like to know how pieces of the wreckage ended up miles away from the crash site; it doesn't make sense at all how any of it got so far away.

To summarize Flight 93 alone:

1. No proof that the terrorists boarded the plane or were in the cockpit.
2. No way that a hijacker could have flown or maneuvered the plane as it was.
3. A false concurrent hijacking that took the attention away from the real one.
4. No proof that Flight 93 actually crashed in the field.
5. An extended debris field (miles away) suggests that the plane possibly broke up in the air.
6. An unexplained small white jet in the area that quickly left the area.
7. The passengers who made calls to loved ones could not have been on the plane, to begin with, so their heroic revolt was a scripted fictional event that fueled a prefabricated legend.
8. Multiple (former military) people heard and recognized a missile strike, suggesting that the plane was shot down.

To summarize 911:

1. Terrorists coordinated on American soil the most sophisticated multi-faceted attack that bypassed the world's biggest Defense Budget.
2. Larry Silverstein buys the Twin Towers just 6 weeks before 9/11.
3. Larry gets a never-before-seen insurance policy for double the value of the buildings with a special policy that specifically covers terrorist attacks. It took 25 different insurance lenders to cover the policy.
4. This was the largest insurance payout in American History.
5. Amazingly, on that specific day, Larry never made it to his daily breakfast appointment in the towers.
6. September 10th, the Pentagon announced that 2.7 trillion dollars were missing funds. The next day, a Boeing 757 plane supposedly hit and destroyed their entire accounting department.
7. Three buildings were hit in less than an hour by radical sand people?
8. Building 7, which was never hit by a plane and sat 1600 feet away from the towers, fell because of office fires? It fell straight down to the ground. Every single

structural engineer calls that impossible and said that it was a controlled demolition.
9. The lead engineer of the towers, Leslie Robertson, said that the towers were specifically designed to withstand the impact of a Boeing 707 airplane.
10. Until 9/11, no steel structure had ever collapsed due to fire, and yet 3 of them happened on this one day.
11. Hundreds of people, including firefighters and police personnel, said that they all heard multiple explosions.
12. Thermite and explosive materials/particles were found in the pulverized remains of the trade center towers by dozens of independent researchers.
13. Why did multiple terrorists have their primary residence/mailing addresses on a U.S. Naval Air Station military base on their driver's licenses?
14. If flight 93 crashed in Shanksville and the FBI said they have 90+ percent of the plane, why have we never been able to see it?
15. Multiple people claim that Flight 93 was shot down if it was the plane that was there at all.
16. Why did N.I.S.T. Admit they deliberately avoided searching for explosive residues in their official investigations?
17. Who were the E-Team (A group of Israeli artists) that were living with unrestricted access to the towers leading up to 9/11?
18. Who were the "Dancing Israelis," and why were they jailed and deported after videotaping and cheering as the towers were hit by planes? They were identified as Israeli Mossad Assets...
19. Why did 100's of top engineers, architects, and experts form an organization to challenge all the lies and narratives from the Government?

7 Questions That Need Answering

1. Why did the owner of the Towers get maximum insurance, which now included Terrorist Attacks 6 weeks before September 11th?
2. Why did the Owner have breakfast in the Towers every morning except on 9/11?
3. The day before 9/11, Donald Rumsfeld said they could not track 2.3 Trillion dollars in transactions, and the records area of the Pentagon just happened to get hit and destroyed.
4. Why was CNN already there and ready to film with a camera crew before the attacks?
5. Why was there an unidentified group of short sales purchased against airline companies right before the attacks?
6. Why was every passenger incinerated in the explosion, and yet the terrorist passport somehow survived?
7. Why was a report published by the Bush Administration a year before 9/11 saying that they needed to aggressively expand Military Power worldwide, but they needed a Massive event to get U.S. and World Wide Support?

12. **Independence Day (July 4th)**: While July 4, 1776, marks the adoption of the Declaration of Independence, the fight for independence from British rule was a lengthy process that began years earlier and involved complex political and social dynamics.

<u>*Here are some notable myths associated with America's 4th of July.*</u>

1. **The Declaration of Independence was signed on July 4th**: While the Continental Congress officially adopted the Declaration on July 4, 1776, most delegates did not sign it until August 2, 1776.

2. **Fireworks were part of the original celebration**: Although fireworks did occur on July 4, 1777, it was not a widespread tradition at the time. The use of fireworks became more common in the years that followed.

3. **Independence Day was celebrated immediately**: The news of the Declaration took time to spread, and celebrations were not uniform across the colonies. Some areas did not recognize it until years later.

4. **John Hancock was the first to sign**: While Hancock is famous for his large signature, he was not the first to sign the Declaration. The signing was done in a somewhat informal manner, and the exact order is not well-documented.

5. **The Fourth of July is a federal holiday due to the Declaration**: Independence Day became an official federal holiday in 1870, long after the Declaration was signed, reflecting the growing national importance of the date.

6. **All Founding Fathers supported the Declaration**: Not all members of the Continental Congress agreed with the Declaration. Some abstained from voting or opposed it for various reasons.

These myths highlight how the historical events surrounding Independence Day have been interpreted and romanticized over time.

13. **Challenger Mission Explosion:** More and more videos have come out showing proof that the Challenger crew members are still alive and working in various fields. They have the same or almost the same names, ages, and extremely close likenesses 30+ years later. They have all been recorded, and numerous interviews have been attempted, but those in question seem to avoid interviews as much as possible. A Brevard County Commission was formed and shows/demonstrates this proof that these astronauts are alive and well. Judith Resnick, Michael J. Smith, and Dick Scobee are three that have been identified.

14. **New Year's Day:** The transition to January 1 as New Year's Day is relatively modern, established by Pope Gregory XIII in 1582. Many cultures celebrate the new year at different times, such as the Lunar New Year or Rosh Hashanah.

1. **Ancient Civilizations**: The earliest recorded New Year celebrations can be traced back to ancient Mesopotamia around 2000 BC, when the new year coincided with the vernal equinox in March. The Babylonians celebrated it with a festival called Akitu, which lasted for several days and involved various rituals, including the crowning of a new king.

2. **Roman Calendar**: In 46 BC, Julius Caesar introduced the Julian calendar, establishing January 1 as the beginning of the year. This change was partly influenced by the Roman devotion to Janus, the god of beginnings and transitions, who was typically depicted with two faces looking both forward and backward.

3. **Medieval Changes**: After the fall of the Roman Empire, the Christian church shifted the date of New Year's celebrations to align with the Feast of the Annunciation (March 25) and later to Christmas (December 25). As a result, January 1 was largely ignored in Europe for several centuries.

4. **Return to January 1**: The Gregorian calendar, introduced by Pope Gregory XIII in 1582, reinstated January 1 as New Year's Day. This reform was adopted by many countries over the following centuries, although some regions retained their traditional dates for a while longer.

5. **Global Celebrations**: Today, New Year's Day is celebrated on January 1 in many countries around the world. However, various cultures have their own New Year celebrations based on their calendars, such as the Chinese New Year, Rosh Hashanah (Jewish New Year), and Diwali (Hindu New Year), each with unique traditions and significance.

15. **COVID-19 Pandemic**: The COVID-19 pandemic was a global health crisis/scam caused by the novel coronavirus SARS-CoV-2, which emerged in late 2019 in Wuhan, China. Supposedly the virus came from bats and or escaped from a level 5 Laboratory and was then used as a bio-weapon against the world. The virus primarily spreads through respiratory droplets and can lead to severe respiratory illness, among other symptoms.

The World Health Organization (WHO) declared COVID-19 a pandemic on March 11, 2020. It led to widespread illness and death, especially when put on hospital respirators, and that overwhelmed healthcare systems worldwide. Governments implemented various measures to control the spread, including lockdowns, travel restrictions, and social distancing. Things were supposedly so bad that places such as The United States Border, Lowes, Home Depot, Walmart etc., were all allowed to remain open, while smaller retailers, churches, and various businesses were forced to shut down.

An extreme amount of people lost their jobs, businesses, homes, family members, and lives, all for the Globalists' narrative. People were censored by all the major social media platforms so that we couldn't mention alternative cures or medications that worked without all the side effects or dying. Ivermectin was one of the possible cures for the extreme flu virus that they call Covid-19. Strange that the Lysol spray has had the Coronavirus labeled on its can for many years.

Vaccination efforts began in late 2020 and were responsible for creating many other health issues for those who became vaccinated, including death. People were forced to get vaccinated in order to keep their employment, even if it was for health reasons, their religion, or just personal choice. The term "My Body, My Choice" no longer had validity. It's strange that it's now 2025, and all the people who were smart enough not to get vaccinated are still alive, and none of them are dead from Covid or its poisonous vaccines.

Also known as the "Fakedemic," as many nations and experts found that the Pandemic was a Fabricated Operation and the Vaccines were a resulting act of Bio-Terrorism. Governments around the world are calling for the immediate ban of the Vaccines and MRNA injections that have been shown to alter human DNA. Many nations have been discussing calls for immediate cuts from ties with the Globalists World Health Organization.

16. **Titanic:** Titanic launched on May 31, 1911, and set sail on its maiden voyage from Southampton on April 10, 1912, with 2,240 passengers and crew on board. On April 15, 1912, after striking an iceberg, the Titanic broke apart and sank to the bottom of the ocean, taking with it the lives of more than 1,500 passengers and crew.

The sinking of the Titanic in 1912 has inspired a variety of conspiracy theories over the years. Here are a few notable ones:

1. **Switch Theory**: One popular theory suggests that the Titanic never sank at all. Instead, it was the Olympic, its sister ship, that went down. Proponents claim that the two ships were switched to claim insurance money, as the Olympic had been damaged in a collision prior to the Titanic's maiden voyage.

2. **Planned Sabotage**: Another theory claims that the sinking was the result of sabotage orchestrated by individuals who opposed the establishment of the Federal Reserve. Some believe that key figures who were against the Federal Reserve were on board and that their deaths were part of a larger plot.

Background: The idea that the sinking was arranged to eliminate key opponents of the Federal Reserve, particularly J.P. Morgan, who had significant financial interests in the ship's operation.

Evidence Cited: Advocates of this theory point to the presence of notable figures on board, such as Isidor Straus and Benjamin Guggenheim, who were opposed to the central banking system. Those who held tickets for a passage, but did not actually sail, include Theodore Dreiser, Henry Clay Frick, Milton S. Hershey, Guglielmo Marconi, John Pierpont Morgan, John Mott, George Washington Vanderbilt II, Edgar Selwyn.

* Some have linked the Rothschild family to the sinking of the Titanic. Stew Peters, a conspiracy theorist, claims that the Rothschilds were responsible for the sinking of the Titanic through a "controlled demolition."

Explanation
The Rothschilds are a wealthy international banking family.

The title of Baron Rothschild is a title in the United Kingdom's Peerage.

The Rothschild family has been involved in many fields, including banking, real estate, mining, energy, agriculture, and winemaking.

Some members of the Rothschild family have held important roles in British public life and business.

3. **The Curse of the Pharaoh**: Some conspiracy theorists link the Titanic tragedy to the supposed curse of ancient Egyptian artifacts that were aboard the ship. They argue that the presence of these artifacts led to a series of misfortunes and, ultimately, the sinking.

4. **Insurance Fraud**: Similar to the switch theory, this idea suggests that the sinking was orchestrated as part of an elaborate insurance fraud scheme. This theory often includes claims that wealthy passengers were in on the plot.

5. **Fire in the Coal Bunker**: A theory posits that a fire in the coal bunker weakened the ship's structure long before it struck the iceberg. Some suggest that this fire was either covered up or ignored by the crew, leading to a catastrophic failure during the voyage.

17. **Sports**: Professional sports were once athletic competitions where hard-trained athletes competed to win the game or contest, and usually, the best person or team won, or you'd get an exciting upset victory. Unfortunately, these days, some of these competitions have so much money backing them or riding on a specific outcome that some of these entertaining athletic sports have just become "Sports Entertainment," where the win will favor the betting odds or the promotions star(s).

There have been several notable instances in sports history where games or competitions were found to be rigged or manipulated. Here are a few examples:

1. **Black Sox Scandal (1919)**: Eight players from the Chicago White Sox conspired to throw the World Series against the Cincinnati Reds for betting purposes. The scandal led to the players being banned from baseball for life.

2. **Sumo Wrestling Scandal (2010)**: Several sumo wrestlers and officials were implicated in a match-fixing scandal in Japan, where it was revealed that some wrestlers were intentionally losing matches in exchange for money.

3. **NBA Referee Scandal (2007)**: Former NBA referee Tim Donaghy was found to have bet on games he officiated and was involved in fixing the outcomes of certain games, compromising the integrity of the league.

4. **Cycling Doping Scandal (Lance Armstrong)**: Lance Armstrong, a seven-time Tour de France winner, was found to have used performance-enhancing drugs and was stripped of his titles. This scandal revealed a culture of doping in professional cycling.

5. **The 2006 Italian Football Scandal (Calciopoli)**: Several top Italian football clubs, including Juventus, AC Milan, and Fiorentina, were found to be involved in a match-fixing scandal, manipulating the appointment of referees to benefit certain teams.

6. **Olympic Scandals (Various)**: There have been multiple instances in Olympic history where athletes have been caught using performance-enhancing drugs, leading to disqualifications and stripped of medals. In some cases, there were allegations of judges being influenced in sports like boxing and gymnastics.

7. **National Football League:** The belief that the NFL (National Football League) is fixed or rigged is a topic among fans. Here are some key points that contribute to this perception:

1. **Referee Controversies**: There have been numerous instances where officiating decisions have been controversial, leading fans to believe that games can be influenced by biased calls. High-profile games, such as the "No Call" in the NFC Championship Game in 2019, have fueled these theories.

2. **Player Injuries**: Some fans speculate that the league may benefit from certain teams or star players being sidelined, impacting viewership and revenue. The management of injuries and the timing of player returns can sometimes lead to skepticism.

3. **Parity and Predictability**: The NFL's salary cap and draft system are designed to promote competitive balance, but this can also lead to predictable outcomes in certain seasons, causing some to question the authenticity of competition.

4. **Betting and Gambling**: With the rise of sports betting, there's a perception that financial interests could influence game outcomes. The NFL has embraced sports betting partnerships, which can lead to concerns about integrity.

5. **Conspiracy Theories**: Some fans point to patterns in game outcomes, playoff matchups, and Super Bowl results as evidence of manipulation. These theories often emerge after unexpected victories or losses.

While these points can generate skepticism, The league maintains that its games are competitive and fair, and investigations into officiating or player conduct are taken seriously.

People's ideas that professional boxing is rigged or corrupt have been questioned for many years. Here are some factors that contribute to this belief:

1. **Judging Controversies:** Boxing matches are often decided by judges, and there have been numerous instances of questionable scoring. Fans and analysts sometimes believe that judges may be influenced by factors like fighter popularity, promotional ties, or even bias, leading to controversial decisions.

2. **Promoter Influence:** Promoters play a significant role in boxing, often having significant power over matchups and fighters. This control can lead to the perception that fights are arranged to benefit certain fighters or to create more lucrative matchups rather than purely based on competitive merit. An example is when Oscar De La Hoya fought in his own promotion and ended up winning a decision that he should have clearly lost against an up-and-coming young boxer.

3. **Match Fixing:** Throughout boxing history, there have been scandals involving match-fixing, where fighters or promoters have colluded to influence the outcome of a bout, often for financial gain. High-profile cases have led to increased scrutiny of the sport. An example would be the 2024 boxing match between Mike Tyson and Jake Paul, where many clear video examples showed that the fight was fixed.

4. **Fighter Health and Safety:** The emphasis on making money can sometimes overshadow concerns about fighter safety. When fighters are pushed to compete despite injuries or other health issues, it raises ethical questions about the integrity of the sport.

5. **High Stakes and Gambling:** The connection between boxing and gambling can create an environment where fixing fights may seem tempting. The potential for large payouts can lead to corruption, and stories of under-the-table deals surface from time to time.

6. **Public Perception and Conspiracy Theories:** Fans often develop conspiracy theories about specific fights or outcomes, especially when an underdog wins, or a favorite loses unexpectedly. This can perpetuate the idea that the sport is not entirely legitimate.

It's important to note that there are many fighters and promoters who are committed to the integrity of the sport. However, instances of corruption and controversy have made it a topic of concern, leading to calls for improved regulations and oversight in the boxing industry.

These examples show the ongoing challenges of maintaining integrity in sports.

7. **Adolf Hitler:** The President of Argentina said that he is releasing all of the confidential information about "Operation Paperclip" and how Adolf Hitler didn't kill himself in a bunker as the Russian forces moved in on him. Hitler is said to have escaped and lived an additional two decades in Vera Loche, Argentina. DNA testing has revealed that the skull fragment in Russia, believed to be Hitler's, actually belongs to a woman, not the German leader. It's said that Hitler had two children while living out his final days. The CIA, FBI, and even Stalin (Russian Leader) had information and knew that Hitler was there in Argentina and died in the mid-1960s.

CHAPTER 19

MEDICAL PROFITS / MEDICINE FOR.. MONEY

The Hippocratic Oath is one of the pledges made by physicians, emphasizing ethical practice and the commitment to patient care.

Unfortunately, many doctors and medical professionals have lost sight of the oath that they all took and have decided that making financial bonuses and getting perks are more important than their oath and the health/lives of their patients. Sadly, the 'pharmaceutical" companies now own these medical professionals, and the goal is to keep anyone and everyone on prescription drugs that may aid one issue but create three or four other issues that require different medications. The evil cycle is endless.

> Moderna CEO confessed to creating the Covid-19 vaccine 2 years before the virus was released to the world. This means that they knew Covid was coming, that it was pre-planned, pre-meditated, and launched on the world for profit and power. God we pray for exposure and justice for Dr. Fauci, Bill Gates, and the pharmaceutical industry in Jesus' name. Amen!

Hospitals have gone to an extremely expensive and very unethical billing practice that sees an unfortunate decline in care/compassion and an emphasis on the many ways they can charge a patient. Medicine is no longer about curing patients, but how much money they can get from each patient. They Say, "A PATIENT CURED IS A PATIENT LOST," and these days, they operate on this quote, and there is little integrity, compassion, or interest in curing patients. It's too bad that they don't realize that with affordable healthcare and people getting cured of their illnesses, there will still be a constant/never-ending supply of patients.

Here's a brief of the Hippocratic Oath's main principles:

1. **Do No Harm**: Physicians pledge to avoid causing harm to patients.
2. **Patient Confidentiality**: Respecting the confidentiality of patient information is crucial.
3. **Beneficence**: The commitment to act in the best interest of the patient.
4. **Justice**: Ensuring fairness and equality in medical treatment.
5. **Professional Integrity**: Maintaining the integrity of the profession and ethical standards.

Modern versions of the oath might include additional commitments related to social justice, respect for all human beings, and the importance of lifelong learning in medicine.

The modern adaptations of the Hippocratic Oath reflect contemporary values and ethics in medicine. While the original oath emphasized principles like non-maleficence (do no harm) and confidentiality, modern versions often include commitments to patient autonomy, social justice, and the importance of evidence-based practice.

One notable example is the Declaration of Geneva, adopted by the World Medical Association, which serves as a modern version of the Hippocratic Oath. It emphasizes the physician's dedication to serving humanity, respecting the autonomy and dignity of patients, and providing competent medical care. Other medical schools may also have their own variations that align with current ethical standards and cultural

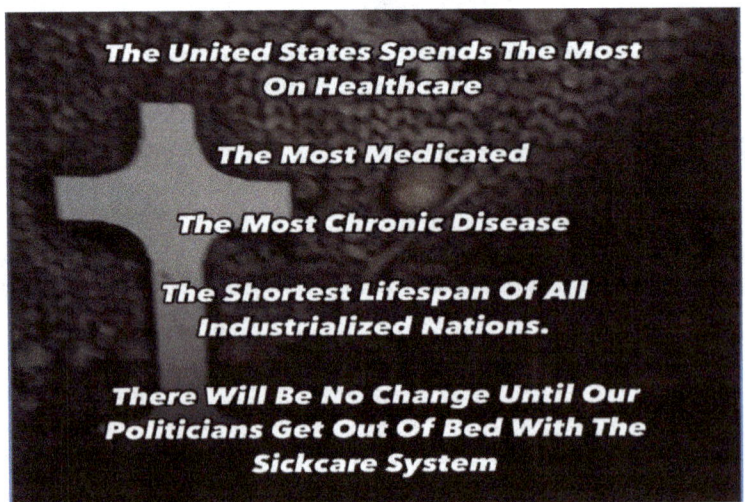

sensitivities. These modern oaths aim to uphold the integrity of the medical profession while adapting to the evolving landscape of healthcare.

Overcharging in healthcare happens in so many ways, leading to significant financial burdens for patients. Here are some examples:

1. **Hospital Charges:** Hospitals often charge exorbitant prices for common procedures. For instance, a standard blood test that costs a few dollars may be billed at hundreds of dollars.

2. **Emergency Room Fees:** Visits to the emergency room can result in high fees, even for minor ailments. Patients may receive bills for facility fees in addition to charges for the physician's services, leading to unexpectedly high total costs.

3. **Surprise Billing:** Patients may receive bills from out-of-network providers who treated them during a hospital stay or emergency situation, which can be significantly higher than in-network rates.

4. **Prescription Drug Prices:** Some medications are marked up significantly, leading to high out-of-pocket costs. Prices can vary widely depending on the pharmacy and insurance coverage.

5. **Diagnostic Imaging:** Procedures like MRIs or CT scans can be overpriced, with costs often inflated compared to the actual market value of the technology and services.

6. **Unbundled Services:** Some providers may charge separately for services that are typically included in a single fee, such as consultations, tests, and follow-up care.

7. **Facility Fees:** Charges for using a facility can be added to the costs of procedures, even if the patient is not receiving any additional services.

Top 5 Politicians Who Have Received the Most Money from Big Pharma

1. Joe Biden - $9,096,598
2. Kamala Harris - $6,162,614
3. Barack Obama - $6,019,863
4. Hillary Clinton - $4,598,860
5. Mitt Romney - $3,356,837

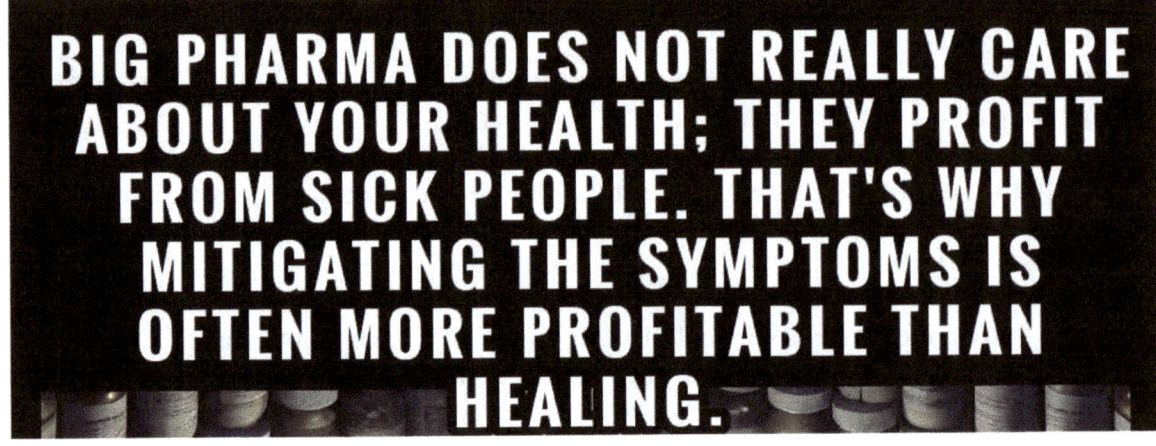

How is this Not a Conflict of Interest??

<u>Vaccines Used to Poison the People</u>

Vaccines are supposedly designed to protect individuals from diseases by stimulating the immune system. The scientific consensus, backed by claims of extensive research and clinical trials, is that vaccines are also supposed to be safe and effective.

REQUIRED VACCINE SCHEDULE
1940: 2 required vaccines
1980: 9 required vaccines
2012: 33 required vaccines
2020: 56 required vaccines
*Birth to Age 18
**Required for entry into school

AUTISM PREVALENCE RATES
1970: 1 in 10,000
1985: 1 in 2500
1995: 1 in 750
2000: 1 in 250
2005: 1 in 166
2015: 1 in 68
2020: 1 in 36

There are many Claims that vaccines are used to harm or poison people (causing Mental or Physical defects such as various degrees of Autism or even Death), and some may say that this stems from misinformation. But after the "Planned Pandemic" of 2020 (COVID-19), it's obvious that Vaccines aren't just for the health benefits of the world's people; they're for "Population Control" and for "Huge Profits" at the risk of many human lives.

The ingredients in flu vaccines can vary depending on the specific type of vaccine, but they generally include the following components:

1. **Inactivated Virus:** Most flu vaccines contain inactivated (killed) viruses that stimulate an immune response without causing the disease.

2. **Live Attenuated Virus:** Some vaccines use a weakened form of the virus, which is usually administered as a nasal spray.

3. **Adjuvants:** These are substances added to enhance the immune response. Not all flu vaccines contain adjuvants.

4. **Stabilizers:** Ingredients like sugars or proteins that help maintain the vaccine's effectiveness during storage.

5. **Preservatives:** Some vaccines may contain preservatives like thimerosal, though many formulations are available in preservative-free versions.

6. **Buffers:** These help maintain the pH of the vaccine.

7. **Residuals:** Small amounts of substances used during the manufacturing process, such as egg proteins (for vaccines produced in eggs), may also be present.

Common side effects of the flu vaccine. They may include:

1. **Soreness at the Injection Site:** This is the most common side effect, often accompanied by redness or swelling.

2. **Fatigue:** Some people may feel tired or fatigued after receiving the vaccine.

3. **Headache:** Mild headaches can occur in some individuals.

4. **Muscle Aches:** General body aches or muscle soreness may be experienced.

5. **Fever:** A low-grade fever can develop as the body builds immunity.

6. **Chills:** Some individuals may experience chills along with fever.

7. **Nausea:** A feeling of nausea may occur in some cases.

The number of people who die from the flu each year can vary based on the severity of the flu season. According to the Centers for Disease Control and Prevention (CDC), estimates indicate that in the U.S., the flu results in:

- Between 12,000 and 52,000 deaths annually.
- Around 140,000 to 810,000 hospitalizations.

Globally, the World Health Organization (WHO) estimates that seasonal influenza epidemics result in about 290,000 to 650,000 respiratory deaths each year. These numbers can fluctuate due to factors such as the virulence of the circulating flu strains, vaccination rates, and public health measures.

Covid-19 Vaccines

The ingredients in COVID-19 vaccines can vary depending on the specific vaccine. Here are the main types of COVID-19 vaccines and their common ingredients:

1. mRNA Vaccines (e.g., Pfizer-BioNTech and Moderna):
   - mRNA: Messenger RNA that provides instructions for cells to produce a protein found on the surface of the virus.
   - Lipids: Fat molecules that help deliver the mRNA into cells.
   - Salts: Such as potassium chloride and sodium chloride, to maintain the pH.
   - Sugar: Such as sucrose, to help stabilize the vaccine.

2. Viral Vector Vaccines (e.g., Johnson & Johnson's Janssen):
   - Modified Viral Vector: A harmless virus (not the coronavirus) that carries genetic material from the coronavirus.
   - Stabilizers: Ingredients to maintain the stability of the vaccine.
   - Salts and Sugars: To help maintain the vaccine's effectiveness.

3. Protein Subunit Vaccines (e.g., Novavax):
   - **Protein Antigens**: Pieces of the virus that stimulate an immune response.
   - Adjuvants: Substances that enhance the immune response (e.g., Matrix-M).
   - Stabilizers and Preservatives: To ensure the vaccine remains effective.

The most common side effects reported after receiving a COVID-19 vaccine are generally mild and temporary. They can include:

1. **Injection Site Reactions:** Soreness, redness, or swelling at the injection site.

2. **Fatigue:** Feeling tired or fatigued is a common response.

3. **Headache:** Many individuals report mild to moderate headaches.

4. **Muscle Pain:** General muscle aches or soreness can occur.

5. **Chills:** Some people may experience chills after vaccination.

6. **Fever:** A low-grade fever may develop as the body builds immunity.

7. **Joint Pain:** Some individuals may experience joint discomfort.

8. **Nausea:** Feeling nauseous can occur in some cases.

As of my last update, COVID-19 has caused millions of deaths worldwide since the pandemic began in late 2019. The exact number can vary depending on the source and the date of reporting, but estimates indicate that over 6 million deaths have been attributed to COVID-19 globally.

It's Amazing how similar the two vaccines are and how they have the exact same side effects. Through much research and with much of my research using AI and Google, I have found that there is definitely a conspiratory narrative to keep much of the truths away and censors any other objective from the people. These platforms are only giving me the information that they want me to believe and attempts to drive me away from other possible and probable truths!

Just a Note:
Vaccines that aren't purposely dangerous don't need their producers to have immunity from lawsuits and prosecution.

Covid History

* Corona Virus has been in play as a biological weapon agent since 1966.
* In 1990, Pfizer filed the first patent on a vaccine for coronavirus.
* 1999 it was modified to cause cardiomyopathy in rabbits.
* 2002 - a patent was filed called the Infectious Replication Defective Clone of Corona Virus.
* 2019 They weaponized Healthcare…

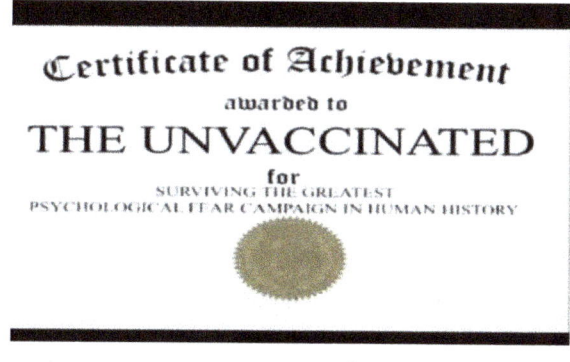

CHAPTER 20

EXPOSING THE GOVERNMENT CORRUPTION

The United States Government has gotten so far out of control that their Tyrannical and Corrupt behavior has led them to do anything to hide their obvious crimes. There is no oversight, so they feel that they can do anything that they want, and when someone threatens to expose them or a Whistleblower comes forward, they somehow just happen to have an accident or a terminal health issue that suddenly takes their lives, they take their own lives, or in one way or another, They Are Silenced!

Here are just a few examples of the Tyranny, Corruption, Lies, and Murderous actions that have been taken by this unchecked government.

The topic of individuals associated with the Clintons who have died under various circumstances has led to numerous conspiracy theories and speculation over the years. There have been many more, but here are some of the more prominent cases.

Speaking of Fraud, a full and extensive criminal investigation by the Maricopa County Sheriff's Office has been concluded and has finally proven that Barak Obama was never an American Citizen and that his birth certificate was a fake. These Federal documents were a fraud carried out by many U.S. Government officials. They lied, cheated, and scammed us all!

Check out **neonplasticlotus.com**

1. **Vince Foster:** A Deputy White House Counsel during the Clinton administration, Foster was found dead in 1993. His death was ruled a suicide, but conspiracy theories have emerged suggesting foul play.

2. **Seth Rich:** A DNC staffer who was murdered in Washington, D.C., in 2016. Some conspiracy theories falsely allege that his death was connected to the Clintons due to his supposed involvement in leaking emails to WikiLeaks.

3. **Ron Brown:** The former Secretary of Commerce died in a plane crash in 1996. There were conspiracy theories suggesting his death was not accidental, especially given that he was set to testify in a scandal involving the Clinton administration.

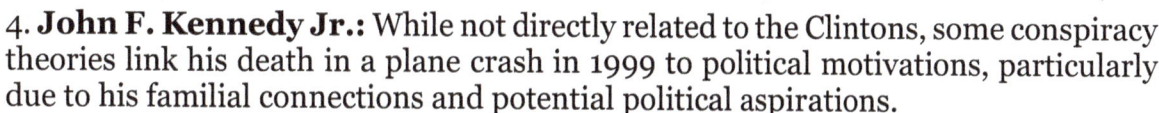

4. **John F. Kennedy Jr.:** While not directly related to the Clintons, some conspiracy theories link his death in a plane crash in 1999 to political motivations, particularly due to his familial connections and potential political aspirations.

5. **Other Cases:** Over the years, various other individuals (over 40) have been mentioned in discussions about mysterious deaths connected to the Clintons, but many of these claims lack credible evidence enough to prosecute them.

1. **Paul Walker:** died just 10 days before he was about to expose the Clinton Foundation for their improprieties in Haiti.
2. **Princess Diana:** had tapes and evidence against the Royal Family involving Pedophilia.
3. **Kobe Bryant:** was said to have damning information and then died first on the Simpson's television show which had the exact year.
4. **Nipsey Hussle:** was about to release a documentary about Dr. Sebi and the cures for Cancer, HIV, AIDS, and more.
5. **Aaliyah:** had information about R. Kelly, Jay Z., Beyonce, and possibly other celebrities.
6. **Avicii:** was gathering evidence against a child porn ring in Hollywood and was working on the documentary "Silent ChildrenDoc."
7. **Amy Winehouse:** was said to be killed because she wouldn't go along with the industry evil doers or sign any more contracts with dirty record labels.
8. **Chris Cornell:** Cornell died in May 2017, and his death was also ruled a suicide by hanging. Some theories surrounding his death suggest that he may have been targeted due to his activism, particularly his involvement in raising awareness about child exploitation and human trafficking. Supporters of this theory point to his vocal criticism of certain powerful figures and organizations and argue that his death could be linked to those positions. Others note that Cornell had a history of substance abuse and mental health issues, which may have contributed to his struggles.

The documentary "Silent Children" explores themes related to child exploitation, trafficking, and the dark underbelly of society that often goes unnoticed.

9. Stanley Meyer: In 1996, Stan created a water-powered car; just two years later, he just happened to be poisoned, and all his information is missing.

While it presents difficult truths, several beliefs have emerged around its content and the broader issues it addresses. Here are some of the conspiracies and theories associated with the documentary:

When voices like JFK, JFK Jr., Trump, Snowden, Elon, Tucker, MLK, Malcolm X, and Assange get silenced or smeared, it makes you wonder - who's the real threat? Them...Or the ones working overtime to shut them up?

1. **Cover-up of Child Trafficking:** Some viewers believe that there is a widespread conspiracy among governments and powerful organizations to hide the prevalence of child trafficking and exploitation. They argue that the media and authorities downplay these issues to protect influential figures.

2. **Hollywood and Pedophilia:** There are conspiracy theories that suggest a connection between Hollywood elites and child exploitation. Some claim that the entertainment industry is involved in covering up or even participating in child trafficking networks.

3. **Ritual Abuse:** Some theories propose that certain groups engage in ritualistic abuse of children, often linked to occult practices. Proponents of this theory suggest that these operations are protected by powerful individuals.

4. **Discrediting Whistleblowers:** There are beliefs that individuals who speak out against child trafficking or exploitation are systematically discredited or **silenced** by powerful interests to prevent them from revealing the truth.

5. **Government Involvement:** Some conspiracy theories suggest that certain government agencies are complicit in child trafficking, either through negligence or active involvement, pointing to historical cases of abuse or exploitation.

Donald J. Trump
@realDonaldTrump

FEMA spent tens of millions of dollars in Democrat areas, disobeying orders, but left the people of North Carolina high and dry. It is now under review and investigation. THE BIDEN RUN FEMA HAS BEEN A DISASTER. FEMA SHOULD BE TERMINATED! IT HAS BEEN SLOW AND TOTALLY INEFFECTIVE. INDIVIDUAL STATES SHOULD HANDLE STORMS, ETC., AS THEY COME. BIG SAVINGS, FAR MORE EFFICIENT!!!

These corrupt government officials continue to commit treason and many other major crimes, like funneling money to other governments and NGOs so that they can get a piece of the pie. They all have decent salaries, but since we allow them to do what they want without oversight or the fear of prosecution, they all somehow become multi-millionaires. This example is where Billions of dollars are sent are sent to Ukraine under the false pretense of "Humanitarian Aid or War support, and then Millions of those dollars come right back to line the pockets of these criminals.

"Nancy Pelosi's husband buys land with federal grants for a high speed rail system from Sacramento to San Diego. Land he couldn't buy was stolen via eminent domain. Pelosi's husband sells the land purchased with federal funds to Diane Feinstein's husband who got federal grant funds to purchase the land from Pelosi's husband. Then he sells the land to the actual developer of the High Speed rail system who purchased it with federal grants. The people of California and the United States purchased the land 3 times making millions of dollars for both the Pelosi and Feinstein families.

USAID gave Chelsea Clinton 84 million dollars, which was supposed to go for Relief in Haiti, but instead, 3 million went to her wedding, and 10 million went to purchase a Luxury Mansion!

Billions of dollars have been stolen at USAID, and other agencies, much of it going to the Fake News Media as a "PayOff" for creating Good News Stories about the Democrats. The Left Wing "Rag," known as Politico, seems to have received $8,000,000.

AMOUNTS OF MONEY UKRAINE HAS BEEN GIVING TO US OFFICIALS

Joe Biden $92M
Mitch McConnell $89M
Nancy Pelosi $86M
Chuck Schumer $66M
Lindsey Graham $82M
Mitt Romney $71M
John Cornyn $41M
Adam Schiff $62M
Dan Crenshaw $20M
Elizabeth Cheney $77M
Kevin McCarthy $42M
Jamie Raskin $38M
Mike Pence $61M
Greg Pence $17M
Rick Scott $63M
Hakeem Jeffries $74M
Ilhan Omar $33M
Elizabeth Warren $42M

U.S. Treasury Department Fraud

February 2025 Report: The U.S. Treasury Department has more waste and abuse of taxpayers' funds than many other departments, with up to 23%... They have people receiving entitlements to the tune of up to 50 Billion dollars a week that have NO known Social Security numbers or identification on record.

Additionally, the Treasury Department has no accountability, doesn't keep itemized records of their payouts, and has no way to check where the money is going! How do they have no formal records of where all that money is going or to whom it's going? If the IRS came to us and asked for itemized records of our income/spending and we didn't have it, they'd assume a large amount and penalize us in a horrible way.

This Government and all its departments are so far out of control that it's insane. They act less like a caring and concerned governing body for their people and the future of their country and more like a criminal organization. How can we be a Nation of Laws when those in elected positions have been breaking all the Laws for decades while prosecuting the common people for lesser crimes?

They all need to be stopped and prosecuted. The number one way to stop these corrupt criminals is to stop providing what they need to operate, which is our tax dollars. If we all stop paying into their slush fund, they can't steal our money and subsequently use our money against us! So the key is for us United States Citizens who work hard for our money to support our families and live an enjoyable life to stop paying all these extorted taxes! The old saying goes, "If you don't feed or stop feeding a cat, it won't come around, or it'll go away." The fact is, we wouldn't be almost 40 Trillion in government debt if our own government wasn't stealing all of our money and giving it away to their friends and fake organizations/causes so they can get their cut.

Not a single one of these assholes is screaming about the corrupt misuse of our tax dollars at USAID. They are only screaming about Trump-appointed Musk exposing it and shutting it down.

You know a political party (democrats) has gone off the deep end with corrupted power when they go above and beyond the law to destroy their political opponent. Here are a few examples of how badly they wanted to keep their false power so that all of their lies, corruption, scandals, and thievery wouldn't get exposed to the world.

* Illegally spied on Trump
* Undermined Trump's presidency, stole the 2020 election.
* Arrested Trump
* Charged Trump
* Indicted Trump
* Gagged Trump
* Censored Trump
* Raided Trump's Private Residence
* Jailed Trumps supporters
* Attempted to remove Trump from State Ballots
* Convicted Trump
* TRIED TO KILL MR. TRUMP.....

* 90 Thousand dollars spent for $100 worth of bushings
* 1.3 Billion was sent to Deceased People, and the checks were actually cashed.
* 59 Million spent on luxury hotels for illegals while Americans are living in tents.

Department of Government Efficiency ✓
@DOGE

Today, @NIH cancelled the following grants:

- $620K for "an LGB+ inclusive teen pregnancy prevention program for transgender boys"
- $699K for studying "cannabis use" among "sexual minority gender diverse individuals"
- $740K for examining "social networks" among "black and Latino sexual minority men in New Jersey"
- $50K for assessing "sexual health" among "LGTBQ+ Latinx youth in an agricultural community"

* 2 Billion in assistance to Taliban Leaders
* 400 Billion Pandemic payments improperly disbursed.
* 15.7 Billion spent to maintain federal buildings with only 25% of capacity used.
* 2.7 Trillion of improper payments in Medicare and Medicaid overseas.
* 600 Million on Sushi.
* $230,000 monthly on Starbucks.
* $1280 per disposable plastic cup for coffee.

10 TRILLION GONE

The US Treasury can't track $4.7 trillion in payments.

Medicare sent $2.7 trillion overseas to people that weren't eligible.

Pentagon lost track $2.5 trillion.

Social Security sends $100 billion a year to people with no identity.

Department of Education spends $50 billion a year to make your kids gay.

USAID spends $50 billion a year to make everybody else gay.

DOGE DISCOVERS USAID SECRETLY FUNNELS $4 BILLION TO BILL GATES PLUS ANOTHER $880 MILLION TO THE WORLD HEALTH ORGANIZATION

* **Joe Biden spent $3 Billion to make 93 Electric Mail Trucks. That's $32 Million for each damn mail truck! Where is the money?**
* **D.O.G.E. Just exposed the U.S. Treasury Department for NOT tracing 4.7 Trillion dollars.**

WASTED
- $29M TO IMPROVE YOUNG EGYPTIANS' SKILLS
- $3.3M FOR LGBTI EXPERIENCE IN CARIBBEAN
- $4.5M TO FIGHT KAZAKHSTAN DISINFORMATION
- $49M TO IMPROVE ZAMBIA SCHOOLS' READING
- $55M FOR LYBIAN FINANCIAL MANAGEMENT
- $59M TO NYC HOTELS FOR HOUSING MIGRANTS

<u>Ways we can make the government more accountable to its citizens.</u>

1. **Transparency:** Implementing policies that require government actions and decisions to be transparent, including public access to documents, meetings, and decision-making processes. This can be facilitated through open data initiatives and citizen approval.

2. **Citizen Engagement:** Encouraging active participation from citizens through public forums, town hall meetings, and online platforms where they can voice concerns, ask questions, and contribute to decision-making processes.

3. **Strengthening Oversight Bodies:** Empowering independent oversight bodies to audit government offices, monitor all activities and spending, scrutinize proposed laws, and ensure strict compliance with current regulations.

4. **Electoral Reforms:** Ensuring fair and transparent electoral processes can lead to government officials being held accountable to legal citizens. This includes any and all campaign finance reform and voting reforms to enhance accessibility and fairness.

5. **Whistleblower Protections:** Establishing and enforcing strong protections for whistleblowers who expose government corruption, misconduct, and illegal activities can act as a deterrent against corruption and promote accountability.

6. **Public Accountability Mechanisms:** Creating mechanisms for citizens to hold officials accountable, such as recall elections, petitions, legal prosecution, or citizen review boards that evaluate government performance.

7. **Education and Awareness:** Promoting civic education to inform citizens of their rights and responsibilities, enabling them to demand accountability and engage with their government effectively.

By combining these approaches, government officials would have less room to engage in illegal activities and citizens can foster a more accountable government that responds to their needs and concerns.

The U.S. Constitution does contain provisions aimed at preventing corruption and ensuring accountability among public officials. Here are some key elements related to corruption:

1. **Impeachment:** Article II, Section 4, states that the President, Vice President, and all civil officers of the United States can be removed from office for "Treason, Bribery, or other high Crimes and Misdemeanors." This provides a mechanism to hold officials accountable for corrupt actions.

2. **Oath of Office:** Article II, Section 1, requires the President to take an oath to "preserve, protect and defend the Constitution of the United States," emphasizing the

expectation of integrity in office. None of these were done during the Obama and Biden years of presidency.

3. **Checks and Balances:** The Constitution establishes a system of checks and balances among the three branches of government (executive, legislative, and judicial) to prevent any one branch from becoming too powerful or corrupt. Unfortunately they all seem to be conspiring together to rule over the citizens of the U.S.

4. **First Amendment Rights:** The First Amendment protects the rights to free speech, assembly, and petition, allowing citizens to express their concerns about corruption and advocate for reform. These rights have been suppressed as the government has used our Social Media platforms to censor us and restrict our First Amendment Rights.

5. **Due Process and Equal Protection:** The Fifth and Fourteenth Amendments ensure that all individuals are entitled to due process and equal protection under the law, which can be invoked in cases of government misconduct or corruption.

While the Constitution lays the groundwork for accountability and integrity within the government, additional laws and regulations have been enacted over time to address corruption, such as campaign finance laws, anti-bribery statutes, and transparency regulations. It's just sad that these laws have been ignored and broken continuously without repercussions.

"A nation of people run by bankers will always be in debt. Just as a nation run by warmongers will never know peace."

President Trump was quoted as saying:

"It looks like billions of dollars have been stolen at USAID and other agencies. Much of it going to the Fake News Media as a Pay-Off for creating good stories about Democrats. The Left Wing Rag known as Politico seems to have received $8,000,000. Did the New York Times receive money??? Who else did??? This could be the biggest scandal of them all, perhaps the biggest in history! The Democrats can't hide from this one; it's too big and too dirty!"

Afraid to be Assassinated by Government Officials

Think about what we've seen in the last 4 years (2020 - 2024) and more importantly, what we've been finding out in the last 6.2 weeks (January 20, 2025 - March 5, 2025)! Our government is nothing but the most powerful and corrupt criminal organization that has many lives buried in the deserts. Anybody who attempts to disclose their evil deeds seems to end up having an accident or decides to suddenly take their own lives.

This is true for both common folks, celebrities who know too much, and even top Political figures / Leaders of countries.

Even now, at least two attempts have been made on the life of Donald Trump for attempting to expose them. Now you have Elon Musk, who is in charge of "D.O.G.E." Department of Government Efficiency, who may have a target on his head for all the corruption and misappropriation of taxpayers money he is showing the world. Crimes that would have any of us common folks arrested, exposed, prosecuted, and in prison for years if we were to do. However, Just to prove the depth of their nefarious power, Elon recently went on the Joe Rogan podcast, and as they were speaking about all the Insider Trading and corruption that's been found so far, he was noticeably afraid to speak about "Everything" that he's found and wouldn't tell Joe.

Elon was quoted as saying that *"what he knows and if he pushes too hard on how they (the corrupt government officials) are acquiring wealth, he's not lengthening his lifespan. By exposing them all and their methods is dangerous because he may get **assassinated**. He has to be careful not to push too hard on the corruption stuff because it's going to get him killed."*

So here is a guy working for the President of these United States to find and expose the trillions of dollars in wasted taxpayer money, and even he is too afraid to investigate and expose all the corruption that our government is doing because he is likely to be killed by these same people! So, as always, **we'll never get the whole truth and expose all their criminal activities** under the **Fear of Death**! Tell me how these criminals are getting away with this? How have we not seen that their power has escalated way out of control, and they all need to be abolished…Immediately!

You can not claim to be a law-abiding nation and expect the citizens to obey the laws of the land when the government itself is the least law-abiding organization, not just in our own country but in the world!

As of 2024, there were at least 340,110,988 people in our population; why the hell are we letting this small amount of thieves to enslave us, control us, kill us, and steal from us?!

Hypocrites is the word that best describes our government; as they say, "We are a nation of laws," and yet they break them all. They imprison people for committing crimes, and yet they commit the same crimes on a much higher level and worse. They are a crime syndicate that has no accountability or oversight. They are the worst of the worst for their hypocritical ways of do what I say, not what I do!

CHAPTER 21

A WORLD OF SUPERSTITIONS, CULTS, SECRET SOCIETIES AND RELIGIONS

Religion - The Great Divide

The one thing that separates the humans of this world is their belief(s) in a higher power or creator(s) of the universe that controls all things, both good and bad. These invisible beings have stories from all nations from ancient times until today. Wars have been started, people have been decimated, and nations have fallen over religion.

However, strangely enough, they all want to pretend to believe in their god(s) and fight wars and hate each other over it, but at the same time they continue to commit evils or sins of the world that they claim are against their religion. That says that they obviously don't truly believe in their god(s) or their ability to make them suffer in their different Hells for those sins.

If they truly believed in the afterlife and the possible punishment(s) each religion claims to have for their indiscretions, then why would they be trafficking children, raping children, involved in prostitution, greed, corruption, along with the many other crimes they commit? The truth of the matter is that they know something that none of us know, or they don't really believe in their own rituals/superstitions, because if they did, then they definitely wouldn't be doing all the evil that they do knowing that life is temporary and they're going to burn for all eternity.

Does all this evil, greed, corruption, and deceitfulness come from generational learning, or is it from the evil religions and practices that the "so-called Elites" are rumored to engage in?

The disturbing actions and practices of these people lead me to believe that either they do not believe in a God or that they have no fear of God and the mysteries of the afterlife. If the churches, pastors, priests, elites, politicians, and celebrities believed that there was something to fear, such as eternal damnation, would they truly act as they do?

It's as though they do not believe that there will be consequences for their evil deeds. Do they truly believe that they can take their money with them?

Cabal: a secret political clique or faction. Cabal comes from the word cabbala (also spelled kabbala), which refers to a Jewish tradition of interpreting texts.

A cabal is a secret plot or a small group of people who create such a plot. Some conspiracy theories are based on the idea that governments worldwide are in the hands of a powerful cabal.

The Cabal was an influential black-aligned organization in Otaria, in Dominaria. Consisting of Clerics, Wizards, and Minions it worshipped money, profit, and the numen Kuberr.

Theories about the cabal and government often revolve around suggestions of secretive groups or organizations manipulating events behind the scenes. Here are some common themes:

1. **Illuminati:** This theory suggests that a secret society, often referred to as the Illuminati, controls world events and governments to establish a **"New World Order."**

2. **Deep State:** The deep state theory suggests that there is a hidden government within the legitimate government, made up of bureaucrats and military officials who are believed to have significant control over policy and national security, often opposing elected officials.

3. **Globalism:** Some theories claim that global elites are working to undermine national sovereignty in favor of a one-world government, often citing organizations like the United Nations or the World Economic Forum.

4. **Financial Control:** Theories in this category claim that a group of wealthy individuals or families manipulates global financial systems for their benefit, influencing governments to implement policies that favor their interests.

5. **Media Manipulation:** Some suggest that mainstream media is controlled by a **cabal** that shapes public perception and opinion to align with the agendas of powerful organizations or governments.

6. **Surveillance and Control:** There are rumors that modern governments are using technology to surveil and control populations, often linking this to a broader agenda of social manipulation and suppression of dissent.

Stories involving secret governments, celebrities, and allegations of horrific practices like drinking children's blood are being told by "whistleblowers" more and more. Here are some of the main ideas associated with these theories:

1. **Satanic Panic:** This theory emerged in the 1980s and 1990s, suggesting that a widespread network of satanic ritual abuse existed involving various high-profile

individuals, including celebrities. These allegations included claims of child abduction and abuse in the context of satanic rituals.

2. **Pizzagate:** This conspiracy theory arose during the 2016 U.S. presidential election, suggesting that a pizzeria in Washington, D.C., was involved in a child trafficking ring linked to prominent politicians and celebrities; the stories gained traction among multiple groups. Secret code words such as **"Pizza"** have been said to be used during interviews and while giving speeches that refer to child trafficking and pedophilia.

The conspiracy theory involving the code word "pizza" is primarily associated with the Pizzagate conspiracy theory that emerged during the 2016 U.S. presidential election. Here's an overview of the theory:

PG1. **Origin:** The Pizzagate theory stems from leaked emails from John Podesta, Hillary Clinton's campaign chairman, which were published by WikiLeaks. Some individuals claimed that certain words in these emails, including **"pizza,"** were code words for human trafficking and pedophilia.

PG2. **Interpretation of Code Words:** Proponents of the theory suggested that "pizza" was used as a euphemism for pedophilia or child exploitation. They alleged that if someone mentioned "pizza" in conversations, it was indicative of involvement in these illicit activities.

PG3. **Connection to Comet Ping Pong:** The theory specifically targeted a Washington, D.C., pizzeria called Comet Ping Pong. Conspiracy theorists alleged that it was the center of a child trafficking ring operated by powerful individuals, including politicians, musicians, and celebrities.

PG4. **Spread of Misinformation:** The theory gained traction on social media, leading to multiple celebrities claiming that this is misinformation. Many entities and individuals decided to investigate and disseminate the many claims.

PG5. **Real-World Consequences:** Despite celebrities' and politicians' claims of the code word "pizza" being false, the Pizzagate conspiracy theory led to real-world consequences, including a man entering Comet Ping Pong with a firearm to "investigate" the claims. Fortunately, no one was harmed, but if the stories have any merit, how many children have been harmed for their evil pleasures?

Overall, the use of "pizza" as a code word in this context reflects how conspiracy theories and whistleblowers can lead to harmful consequences based on facts or fictitious claims.

3. **Adrenochrome:** Some conspiracy theorists believe that a substance called adrenochrome, which is supposedly derived from the adrenal glands of living children, is harvested and consumed by elite individuals, including government

officials and celebrities, for its purported psychoactive effects and life-extending properties.

4. **Hollywood Elites and Pedophilia:** There are unfounded theories suggesting that many Hollywood stars and industry leaders participate in or cover up pedophilia and human trafficking rings, often citing vague anecdotes or unverified claims.

5. **Occult Practices:** Some theories suggest that certain celebrities are involved in occult practices, including blood rituals or sacrifices, as part of their rise to fame or as a means of maintaining power within a secretive elite.

6. **Distraction from Real Issues:** A common thread in many of these theories is the idea that they serve as distractions from systemic issues within society, such as inequality, corruption, and abuse of power.

7. **QAnon:** This theory alleges that a secret cabal of Satan-worshipping pedophiles is operating within the U.S. government and other institutions and that during his first term, President Donald Trump was working to expose and defeat them. QAnon gained significant attention and followers, particularly during the 2020 election cycle.

The various Celebrity and Elite Theories suggest that celebrities and elite individuals are involved in secret societies, human trafficking, or occult practices, often linking them to claims of pedophilia or satanic rituals.

Stories regarding celebrities and politicians performing satanic rituals often stem from a mix of whistleblowers, folklore, urban legends, and the media. Here are some of the common stories associated with these theories:

1. **Blood Sacrifices:** Some theorists claim that politicians and other high-profile individuals engage in rituals that involve the sacrifice of animals or even humans as a means of gaining power, fame, or influence.

2. **Occult Practices:** There are stories that politicians and celebrities participate in occult ceremonies, often involving symbols associated with satanism, such as the use of pentagrams, inverted crosses, or other esoteric symbols. We've seen some of these possible symbols on politicians and celebrities during interviews.

3. **Baphomet Worship:** Baphomet, a figure often associated with occultism and satanism, is claimed by some conspiracy theorists to be worshipped by political elites as a representation of power and knowledge.

4. **Illuminati Rituals:** Theories suggest that members of the Illuminati or other secret societies perform rituals to solidify their control over the entertainment industry and political landscape, often associating these rituals with satanic themes.

5. **Hollywood Parties:** Some stories say that exclusive Hollywood parties are fronts for satanic rituals, where attendees engage in debauchery and occult practices, often linked to drug use and sexual exploitation.

6. **Symbolism in Media:** People often point to music videos, movie scenes, and public appearances that feature occult symbolism as evidence that celebrities are part of a larger satanic agenda. Are these symbols fact or fiction? We may never know the truth, but whistleblowers claim that they are factual.

7. **Mind Control:** Some theories suggest that satanic rituals are used for mind control purposes, with the aim of conditioning individuals to serve the interests of powerful politicians and Hollywood elites.

*Regardless of what they practice or believe, **Proverbs 29:4-11** emphasizes the importance of justice and righteousness in leadership.*

It warns that a King/Leader who accepts bribes and acts unjustly, just as all these Politicians do on a daily basis, will destroy their nation, while A righteous leader will bring stability; it also highlights the contrast between the behavior of the wicked, who are easily caught in their own traps.

CHAPTER 22

TAXING AMERICANS INTO POVERTY
(FOOD, GAS, HOUSING, TAXATION)

Why are we Over-Taxed for being Productive Members of Society?

It's stated that "Taxation without Representation is Theft," and that's exactly what we have here in the United States. Billions of (American Tax) dollars go out each year to house, feed, clothe, and give healthcare to foreign countries while American veterans/citizens starve, become homeless, are sick, and get ignored by the Government.

Who pays for all this? The working class of the American people, that's who. We work our asses of day in and day out and then get taxed for more and more every year just so the corrupt, tyrannical government can have an unlimited supply of money to pass around to their friends and themselves.

It's ridiculous that every year, they spend so much money on television and radio advertisements to attempt to make getting your taxes done seem so much fun. So how fun is it now that you are all finally seeing that you pay so much in extorted taxes that you can fund perverted and immoral programs in foreign countries?

Americans have now let the government get so out of control that they've allowed them to tax us for everything. All these ways to tax us through the overabundance of Insurance and taxes. We have to have Insurance for almost everything and these companies just keep raising the rates on us, and soon, we'll not be able to afford anything. I'm surprised (and it's probably coming soon) that the government hasn't mandated or made into law that we all have to have Life Insurance where they'll be automatically named as a partial beneficiary. That way, when each of us dies, they'll still be able to collect from us one last time!

At Least 50 Different ways the Government Steals from you, the American Citizen, in the form of Taxes while giving away your hard-earned money to foreign nations, foreign nationals, foreign contractors, and themselves.

1. **Federal Income Tax** - Tax on individual income at progressive rates.
2. **State Income Tax** - Varies by state, taxing individual income.
3. **Local Income Tax** - Taxes imposed by cities or counties on income.
4. **Social Security Tax** - Payroll tax funding Social Security benefits.
5. **Medicare Tax** - Payroll tax funding Medicare health insurance.
6. **Capital Gains Tax** - Tax on profits from the sale of assets.
7. **Dividend Tax** - Tax on dividends received from investments.
8. **Corporate Income Tax** - Tax on corporate profits.
9. **Sales Tax** - Tax on the sale of goods and services.
10. **Property Tax** - Tax on real estate property value.
11. **Estate Tax** - Tax on the transfer of the estate of a deceased person.
12. **Gift Tax** - Tax on gifts exceeding a certain amount.
13. **Excise Tax** - Tax on specific goods (e.g., alcohol, tobacco).
14. **Luxury Tax** - Tax on high-cost luxury items.
15. **Fuel Tax** - Tax on the sale of gasoline and diesel fuel.
16. **Toll Road Fees** - Charges for using certain roads and bridges.
17. **Utility Taxes** - Taxes imposed on utility services like electricity and water.
18. **Inheritance Tax** - Tax on assets inherited from a deceased person.
19. **Severance Tax** - Tax on the extraction of natural resources.
20. **Insurance Premium Tax** - Tax on premiums paid for insurance policies.
21. **Environmental Taxes** - Taxes on activities that harm the environment.
22. **Cigarette Tax** - Specific tax on cigarette sales.
23. **Alcohol Tax** - Tax on the sale of alcoholic beverages.
24. **Bank Transaction Tax** - Tax on financial transactions made by banks.
25. **Internet Sales Tax** - Tax on online purchases, varying by state.
26. **Payroll Tax** - Taxes withheld from employee wages for social programs.

27. **Self-Employment Tax** - Tax for self-employed individuals covering Social Security and Medicare.
28. **Alternative Minimum Tax (AMT)** - Ensures high-income earners pay a minimum tax.
29. **Foreign Income Tax** - Tax on income earned outside the U.S.
30. **Sales and Use Tax** - Tax on goods purchased out of state but used within the state.
31. **Transportation Tax** - Taxes specifically for funding transportation projects.
32. **Documentary Stamp Tax** - Tax on certain legal documents.
33. **Vehicle Registration Tax** - Tax on registering a vehicle.
34. **Pet Tax** - Some municipalities charge taxes on pet ownership.
35. **Business License Tax** - Tax for obtaining a business operation license.
36. **Franchise Tax** - Tax on businesses operating in a state.
37. **Occupational Tax** - Tax on specific professions or occupations.
38. **Amusement Tax** - Tax on entertainment and amusement activities.
39. **Telecommunication Tax** - Tax on telecommunications services.
40. **Cable Television Tax** - Tax on cable service subscriptions.
41. **Hotel Tax** - Tax on lodging and accommodations.
42. **Transient Occupancy Tax** - Tax on short-term rentals.
43. **Surtax** - Additional tax on certain income levels or activities.
44. **Windfall Profits Tax** - Tax on excess profits, often from natural resources.
45. **Nutritional Tax** - Taxes on sugary drinks or unhealthy food options.
46. **Mansion Tax** - Tax on luxury real estate purchases.
47. **Foreign Bank Account Tax** - Tax on foreign financial accounts.
48. **Carbon Tax** - Tax on carbon emissions intended to reduce greenhouse gases.
49. **Tax on Cryptocurrency Transactions** - Tax on gains from cryptocurrency trades.
50. **Local Business Improvement District Tax** - Tax for funding local business development projects.

These taxes and more reflect the diverse/various ways in which Americans are robbed by the government to cover federal, state, and local revenues. This is how they have Billions of your dollars to just give away in foreign aid to their friends and supporters in foreign countries such as Israel, Ukraine, Pakistan, Egypt, Jordan, Afghanistan, Iraq, South Sudan, Ethiopia, Honduras, Nigeria, Lebanon, Columbia, Bangladesh, and Syria - all while American veterans and citizens are starving, homeless and without medical care.

We Americans who work to make all this money can't afford to live, but government officials and their foreign associates certainly are living well off the skin of our backs! This gross Misappropriation of American funds needs to stop immediately. American citizens and America (the country) are going to shit while government officials and non-Americans prosper. We must end this over-taxation, and all funds need to be allocated to America and Americans only!

A few ways your Extorted/Stolen Tax Dollars are being Wasted!

1. 1.4 million - National Bubble Wrap Stress Relief Program.
2. $900,000 - The Bureau of Mailbox Feng Shui.
   2.3 million - Federal Balloon Animal Training Academy.
3. $600,000 - National Pretzel and Twisting Initiative.
4. 1.8 million - Department of Sock Pairing.
5. 1.2 million - The Federal High Five Coordination Bureau.
6. $700,000 - National Ice Cream Structural Integrity Lab.
7. 3 million - The Office of Puddle Depth Measurement.
8. 1.5 million - Bureau of Alarm Clock Testing.
9. 2 million - Federal Glitter Clean Up Task Force.
10. 20 million - Sesame Street in Iraq.
11. 2 million for Moroccan Pottery classes.
12. 11 million to tell Vietnam to stop burning trash.
13. 27 million to give gift bags to illegal aliens before being deported.
14. Millions to Afghanis to grow crops instead of Opium.
15. 300 million to Afghanis to build diesel fuel power plants that they couldn't use because diesel was too expensive.
16. 200 million on a dam that was too unsafe to ever be used.
17. 250 million on a road that was never used.
18. 9 million to Syrians for humanitarian aid, which ended up going to Al Qaeda.
19. 1 million for bat research in Wuhan.
20. Funded Fashion Week in Paris, France.
21. $100,000 to find out if some fish get more aggressive when given gin or tequila.
22. $700,000 to find out the exact words of Neil Armstrong when he walked on the moon.
23. 120,000 to find out why prisoners want to get out of jail.
24. 1.5 million to encourage people in New York to play more video games.

25. $70,000 spent by Andrew McCabe for a conference table for the Justice Department.
26. 50 million to provide condoms for Gaza.
27. The U.S. Treasury Department doesn't even keep track (supposedly) of where Billions of dollars (Annually) in payments have been paid out to.
28. Millions of dollars to research "Transgender animals," poisoning puppies and testing them on Party Drugs.

The U.S. Government is extorting, stealing, and wasting your money on ridiculous spending on things where they can launder money and make themselves rich through "Kickbacks."

U.S.A.I.D. Is a $40,000,000,000 Deep State Slush Fund for Social Justice!

ALL FOREIGN AID MUST END / AMERICA FIRST

The American government spends so much of its citizens' money on foreign aid that they've completely forgotten about their own country's needs and people, the ones who are actually working and earning the money.

The United States provides financial assistance to various countries for different purposes, including economic development, military support, and humanitarian aid. Here's a list of some countries that the U.S. supports:

1. **Israel** - Significant military and economic aid.
2. **Egypt** - Military and economic support.
3. **Jordan** - Economic assistance and military support.
4. **Afghanistan** - Economic and military aid, especially post-9/11.
5. **Pakistan** - Military and economic assistance.
6. **Ukraine** - Military and economic support, particularly since the U.S. encouraged conflict with Russia.
7. **South Sudan** - Humanitarian assistance and support for peacekeeping.
8. **Ethiopia** - Humanitarian aid and development assistance.
9. **Honduras** - Economic and development assistance.
10. **Bangladesh** - Humanitarian aid and development support.
11. **Nigeria** -
12. **Lebanon** - Disaster Relief, Education and Youth Programs, Democracy and Governance, Security Assistance.
13. **Columbia** - Security Assistance, Economic, Counter-Narcotics Programs and Humanitarian Aid.
14. **Syria** - Humanitarian Assistance.
15. **Iraq** - Security, Economic and Humanitarian Aid.

This list is not exhaustive, as the U.S. provides assistance to many other countries based on strategic interests and humanitarian needs. If you notice, our money and from our tax dollars provide all the things for foreign nations that Americans need. They're giving your money to others instead of providing for our people and country's needs. Many of these countries hate America and wish us dead, and yet we provide our hard-earned money for their safety, security, housing, food, medical aid, education, and existence!

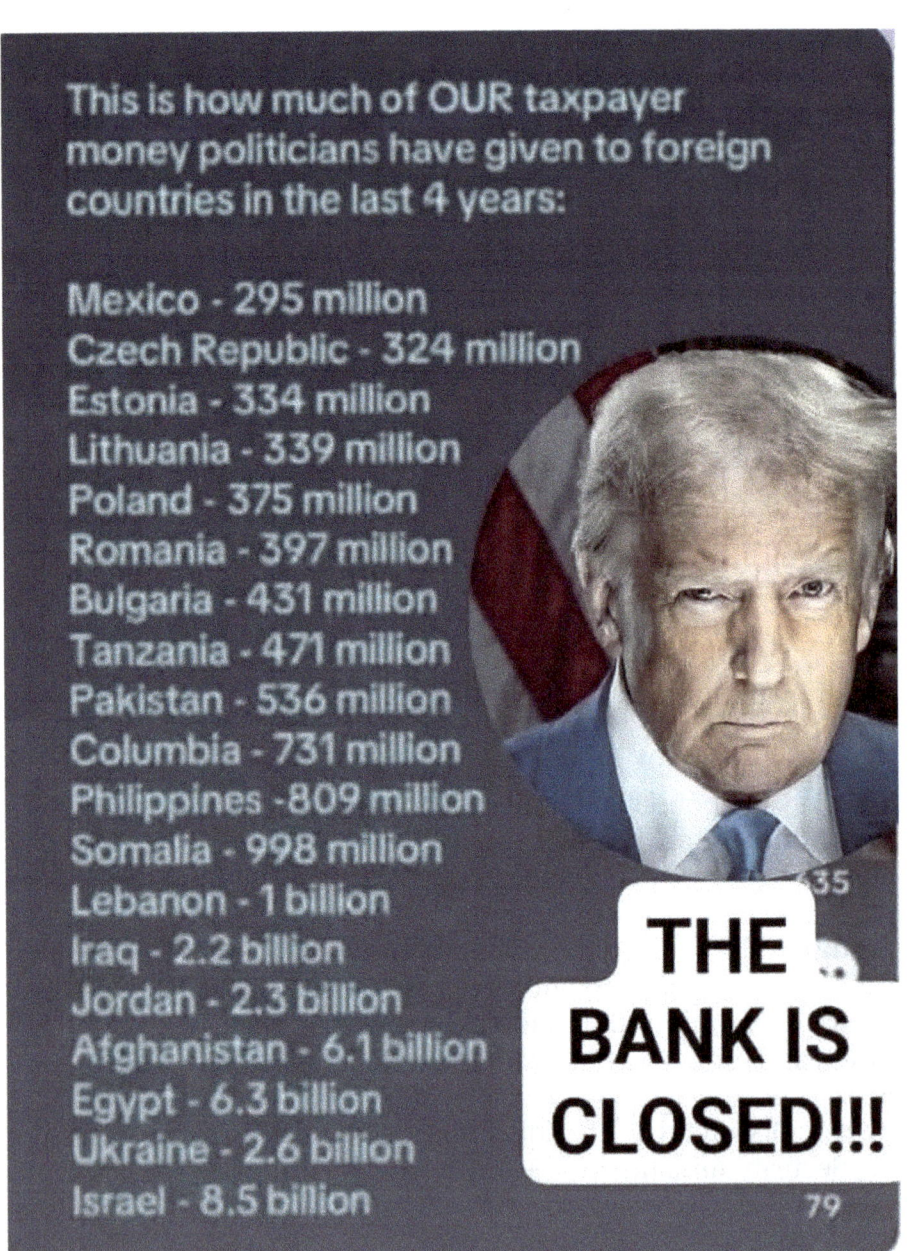

U.S. National Debt

As of January 10, 2025, the U.S. national debt was $36.17 trillion. This is the total amount of outstanding borrowing by the federal government and clearly shows that the U.S. Government can't and shouldn't manage our money or have free unrestricted access / spending power over our Tax Dollars.

Explanation:

* The national debt is the total amount of outstanding borrowing by the U.S. federal government.

* The debt has been increasing, and by November 2024, it reached $36 trillion.

* The debt has doubled over the past 15 years.

* The interest paid on the debt is the fastest-growing part of the budget.

* The debt is a concern because of the higher interest rate environment and how it affects debt repayment.

These undisciplined and uncontrolled spenders are the same people that pass judgment upon us citizens of whether or not we are credit-worthy or not, for things such as homes, cars or other loans, and yet they cannot budget their own spending. We get extorted, audited, judged, and can possibly lose everything and or possibly go to jail for mismanaging your finances.

Maybe if we stop the corruption and wasting all of our American Tax dollars on "Foreign Aid" and taking better care of others rather than our own country and citizens, then I'm sure this debt situation could get under control.

Item	Change
GASOLINE	46.6%
FUEL OIL	59.1%
NATURAL GAS	28.1%
USED AUTOS	26.4%
BEEF	20.1%
PORK	14.1%
BACON	15.4%
CHICKEN	8.8%
EGGS	11.6%
MILK	4.3%
APPLES	6.7%
COFFEE	4.7%
BABY FOOD	7.9%
ELECTRICITY	6.5%

The Truths they Don't Want US to Know

* In China, you pay property tax one time, and then it's your house for life.
* In China you pay a vehicle tax one time and don't have to register it every year.
* If you make under a certain amount of money, you don't pay income tax; they take it from the rich.
* All parks and zoos are FREE because they're public property.
* For only $20 U.S. dollars, you can buy a week's worth of groceries.

Pricing Us into Starvation with Grocery Prices

First they poison our foods, and then Grocery prices have risen due to government Greed, corruption, and a combination of other factors:

1. **Supply Chain Disruptions:** Events like the COVID-19 "Plandemic" disrupted production and distribution, leading to shortages and increased costs.

2. **Inflation:** General inflation affects the cost of goods, including food. Rising costs for labor, transportation, and raw materials contribute to higher prices.

3. **Increased Demand:** Changes in consumer behavior, such as stockpiling or increased demand for certain products, can drive prices up, but this isn't the case.

4. **Weather and Climate Change:** Natural disasters and changing weather patterns can impact crop yields, resulting in reduced supply and higher prices.

5. **Global Issues:** Geopolitical tensions, trade policies, and other global events can affect food availability and prices.

These factors are really just possibilities, but we have $12 for a dozen eggs, $5 per gallon of gas, and way over-priced groceries because of government corruption and greed.

Since our government is doing everything they can to hurt us and drain every penny from our hard-working citizens, Here are some common methods people can use to save on grocery shopping:

1. **Create a Shopping List:** Planning meals and making a list helps avoid impulse buys and stick to necessary items.

2. **Use Coupons and Discounts:** Taking advantage of coupons, digital discounts, and promotional offers can significantly reduce costs.

3. **Buy in Bulk:** Purchasing items in bulk can save money, especially for non-perishable goods.

4. **Shop Sales:** Keeping an eye on weekly sales and discounts can help in buying items at lower prices.

5. **Choose Store Brands:** Generic or store-brand products are often cheaper than name brands but can offer similar quality.

6. **Plan Meals Around Sales:** Adjusting meal plans based on what's on sale can help maximize savings.

7. **Avoid Pre-Packaged Foods:** Preparing meals from scratch is usually cheaper than buying pre-packaged or convenience foods.

8. **Use Loyalty Programs:** Many grocery stores have loyalty programs that offer additional discounts and rewards.

9. **Compare Prices:** Checking prices at different stores or using price comparison apps can help find better deals.

10. **Limit Shopping Frequency:** Reducing the number of grocery trips can help minimize impulse purchases and save money over time.

We shouldn't have to go to these extremes as food should be inexpensive for all to eat, but using these strategies can help maximize savings while grocery shopping.

Government corruption and greed can impact food prices in several ways:

1. **Subsidy Misallocation:** Corruption can lead to misallocation of agricultural subsidies, favoring certain businesses or individuals rather than supporting small farmers, which can distort market competition and inflate prices.

2. **Price Fixing:** In some cases, corrupt practices can lead to collusion among suppliers or retailers to fix prices, artificially raising costs for consumers.

3. **Regulatory Capture:** When regulatory agencies are influenced by powerful agricultural lobbies, policies may be implemented that benefit a few at the expense of the broader market, leading to higher prices.

4. **Tax Evasion and Bribery:** Corruption can result in tax evasion by large corporations, shifting the tax burden to consumers and contributing to higher prices for food products.

5. **Inefficient Supply Chains:** Corruption can lead to inefficiencies in the supply chain, increasing costs in transportation and distribution, which are ultimately passed on to consumers.

6. **Land Grabs and Displacement:** Corruption can facilitate land grabs, displacing small farmers and reducing local food production, which can lead to increased dependence on imports and higher prices.

7. **Inflation and Economic Instability:** Corruption can contribute to broader economic instability, leading to inflation that affects food prices directly.

These factors illustrate how corruption and greed can create a cycle that increases food prices and impacts food security.

Over the years, there have been instances where many IRS employees were found not to be paying their taxes. According to reports from the Treasury Inspector General for Tax Administration (TIGTA), it was revealed that a small percentage of IRS employees had tax delinquencies. For example, a report in 2019 indicated that around 2% of IRS employees were found to have unpaid federal taxes. The amount of non-tax paying IRS employees has grown to a staggering amount in 2024, proving that a stronger oversight protocols need to be in place.

These findings often lead to discussions about accountability and the importance of tax compliance, especially for employees of the agency responsible for tax collection.

Tax compliance can differ between government employees and private sector workers in several ways:

1. **Income Reporting:** Government employees typically have their income reported to the IRS through Form W-2, just like private sector workers. However, government agencies may have more structured payroll systems, which can lead to more accurate withholding and reporting.

2. **Audits and Oversight:** Government employees may be subject to greater scrutiny due to the public nature of their employment. There may be higher expectations for compliance, and violations can have more immediate repercussions, including disciplinary actions.

3. **Tax Benefits and Deductions:** Government employees might have access to specific tax benefits, such as certain retirement plans or health benefits, which can impact their overall tax liability. Private sector workers may have different benefits based on their employer's offerings.

4. **Financial Transparency:** Government employees may be more aware of tax laws and compliance due to training and the nature of their work. This could lead to higher compliance rates compared to private sector workers, who might have varying levels of knowledge about tax obligations.

5. **Enforcement and Penalties:** While both sectors face penalties for non-compliance, the consequences for government employees could be more pronounced, including potential job loss or legal action due to the nature of their public service roles.

6. **Access to Resources:** Government employees might have better access to resources and guidance on tax compliance, given the resources their agencies provide. In contrast, private sector workers may rely more on external tax preparation services or software.

Overall, while both sectors are subject to the same tax laws, the context of their employment can influence their compliance behaviors and the consequences they face for non-compliance.

Forced Insurances
Another way to Tax Americans and get their Kickback

Insurance takes away "Personal Responsibility," and the government uses this tool to force more money out of people like an additional "Tax" by making laws that state that each and every American must have various types of insurance for their lives. It's ridiculous to have mandatory insurance that the government/Insurance Agency can raise prices on at any time. Once again, this is just another way to drain the money out of hard-working Americans.

Here are several types of insurance that are often mandatory or highly recommended for individuals and businesses:

1. **Health Insurance:** Required under the Affordable Care Act (ACA) for most Americans, though there are exemptions. Employers with 50 or more employees must provide health insurance.

2. **Auto Insurance:** Nearly all states require drivers to have some form of auto insurance, which typically includes liability coverage.

3. **Homeowners Insurance:** While not legally required, mortgage lenders often require homeowners to carry insurance to protect against damages to the property.

4. **Workers' Compensation Insurance:** Required for most businesses with employees, this insurance covers medical costs and disability benefits if employees are injured on the job.

5. **Liability Insurance:** Certain professions, like doctors and lawyers, may be required to carry malpractice insurance to protect against claims of negligence.

6. **Disability Insurance:** Some employers may offer disability insurance as part of their benefits package, and in some cases, it may be required.

7. **Flood Insurance:** Required for homes in flood-prone areas if the mortgage is backed by a federal agency.

8. **Umbrella Insurance:** While not mandatory, some states may require it for certain businesses or high-risk individuals.

These requirements can vary by state and specific circumstances, but most of these are just money scams that are required under law so the politicians can get their kickbacks.

Other Individual Insurance Types:

1. **Life Insurance:** Provides financial support to beneficiaries upon the policyholder's death.
2. **Renters Insurance:** Covers personal property in rented spaces.
3. **Long-Term Care Insurance:** Covers long-term care services not covered by health insurance.
4. **Travel Insurance:** Covers financial losses related to travel, such as trip cancellations or medical emergencies.
5. **Umbrella Insurance:** Provides additional liability coverage beyond other policies.
6. **Pet Insurance:** Covers veterinary expenses for pets.

7. **Flood Insurance:** Covers damages specifically from flooding.

8. **Earthquake Insurance:** Covers damages from earthquakes.
9. **Marine Insurance:** Covers loss or damage of ships and cargo.
10. **Builder's Risk Insurance:** Protects buildings under construction.
11. **Fine Arts Insurance:** Covers loss or damage to valuable art pieces.

Business Insurance Types:

1. **General Liability Insurance:** Covers legal liabilities for bodily injury and property damage.
2. **Professional Liability Insurance:** Protects against claims of negligence or malpractice.
3. **Commercial Property Insurance:** Covers damage to business property.
4. **Workers' Compensation Insurance:** Provides wage replacement and medical benefits to employees injured on the job.
5. **Business Interruption Insurance:** Covers lost income due to disruptions in business operations.
6. **Cyber Liability Insurance:** Protects against data breaches and cyberattacks.
7. **Product Liability Insurance:** Covers legal claims related to product defects.
8. **Commercial Auto Insurance:** Covers vehicles used for business purposes.
9. **Directors and Officers (D&O) Insurance:** Protects company directors and officers from legal claims.
10. **Employment Practices Liability Insurance (EPLI):** Covers claims related to employment practices, such as discrimination or wrongful termination.

This list shows a variety of insurance types that can be tailored to meet the specific needs of individuals and businesses in America.

__Forced Licensing__
More Extorted Money from a Greedy Government

In the United States, certain licenses are forced/required by law for citizens to engage in specific activities or professions. Here's a basic list of the licenses that Americans may be required to obtain:

1. **Driver's License:** Required to operate a motor vehicle.
2. **Business License:** Necessary for operating a business legally within a specific jurisdiction.
3. **Professional Licenses:** Required for various professions, including:
   - **Medical Licenses** (Doctors, Nurses)
   - **Legal Licenses** (Lawyers)
   - **Teaching Licenses** (Educators)
   - **Real Estate Licenses** (Realtors)
   - **Accounting Licenses** (CPAs)
   - **Cosmetology Licenses** (Hairdressers, Estheticians)
4. **Building Permits:** Required for construction or significant renovations.

5. **Alcohol License:** Necessary for selling or serving alcoholic beverages.
6. **Firearm License:** Required in many states for purchasing or carrying firearms.
7. **Hunting and Fishing Licenses:** Required for participating in these activities.
8. **Marriage License:** Required to legally marry in most jurisdictions.
9. **Concealed Carry License:** Required to carry a concealed weapon in many states. This and #6 shouldn't be needed as everyone should have the right to bear arms without being controlled in any way by the government…

The **right to bear arms** is the right of **U.S. citizens** to own weapons, as protected by the **Second Amendment** of the **U.S. Constitution**. The amendment was ratified in 1791.

Purpose
The right to bear arms is intended to protect people, their property, and their rights from nefarious individuals or a tyrannical government.

It is also used for hunting and sporting activities.
Supreme Court rulings

In Heller v. District of Columbia, the Supreme Court ruled that the Second Amendment protects the **right to own firearms** for **self-defense**, at least in the home.
In McDonald v. City of Chicago, the Supreme Court ruled that the right to bear arms is a **fundamental right**.

Interpretations
The Second Amendment protects the right to all types of bearable arms, **including those that were not in existence when the Constitution was written.**

The right to bear arms is a fundamental right that is essential to maintaining other rights.

Professional licenses are essential in various fields to ensure that individuals meet specific standards of competency and ethics. Here are some common types of professional licenses required in different fields:

1. **Healthcare:**
   - **Medical License:** Physicians and surgeons must be licensed to practice medicine.
   - **Nursing License:** Registered nurses (RNs) and licensed practical nurses (LPNs) require licensure.
   - **Pharmacy License:** Pharmacists must be licensed to dispense medications.
   - **Physical Therapy License:** Required for physical therapists to practice.

2. **Legal:**

- **Bar License:** Lawyers must pass the bar exam and obtain a license to practice law in their state.

3. **Education:**
   - **Teaching License:** Educators in public schools need to be licensed, often requiring a degree and passing exams.

4. **Finance:**
   - **Certified Public Accountant (CPA):** Accountants must pass exams and meet specific educational requirements.
   - **Financial Advisor License:** Certain licenses, like the Series 7 or Series 65, are needed for financial advisors.

5. **Real Estate:**
   - **Real Estate License:** Required for real estate agents and brokers to buy, sell, or lease property.

6. **Construction and Trades:**
   - **Contractor License:** General contractors and specialized trades (like electricians and plumbers) often need a license.
   - **Home Inspector License:** Required for those inspecting homes for buyers or sellers.

7. **Cosmetology:**
   - **Cosmetology License:** Required for hairdressers, nail technicians, and estheticians.

8. **Engineering:**
   - **Professional Engineer (PE) License:** Engineers must pass exams and meet experience requirements to offer their services to the public.

9. **Technology:**
   - **Certified Information Systems Security Professional (CISSP):** A license for cybersecurity professionals.

10. **Transportation:**
    - **Commercial Driver's License (CDL):** Required for drivers of large or commercial vehicles.

There are several licenses that some individuals and groups debate the necessity of, arguing that they may be overly burdensome or restrictive. Here are a few examples:

1. **Occupational Licenses:** Many argue that certain jobs, such as interior decorators, makeup artists, or pet groomers, do not require formal licenses, suggesting that these professions should be accessible without regulatory barriers.

2. **Business Licenses:** Small business owners sometimes feel that the process to obtain a business license is unnecessarily complex and costly, especially for home-based or freelance businesses.

3. **Fishing and Hunting Licenses:** Some individuals believe that these licenses should not be required for recreational activities, arguing that they restrict access to natural resources.

4. **Marriage Licenses:** There is a debate about the necessity of government-issued marriage licenses, with some advocating for the freedom to marry without state intervention.

5. **Health and Fitness Certifications:** Personal trainers and fitness instructors may face licensing requirements that some argue are excessive, especially if they have relevant experience and knowledge.

6. **Cosmetology Licenses:** Critics argue that the extensive requirements for cosmetology licenses can create barriers to entry into the profession, particularly for individuals with practical skills.

7. **Concealed Carry Permits:** Some advocates for gun rights argue against the need for permits to carry concealed firearms, citing concerns over personal freedom and Second Amendment rights.

8. **Public Speaking or Life Coaching Licenses:** There is a debate about whether individuals should need formal certification to provide guidance or coaching in these areas, as many feel it should be based on experience rather than regulation.

These discussions often center around the balance between ensuring public safety and allowing individuals the freedom to pursue their chosen professions or activities without excessive government regulation.

Requirements can vary by state and locality, whereas some States (California) require a ridiculous amount of licenses for everything and anything. Almost all of these licenses are mandatory and must be renewed on a yearly basis, and most are an absolutely ridiculous way to drain the wallets of its citizens.

I can see why a doctor who is involved in the health and lives of other individuals may need a license, but you may ask yourself why they need to be renewed every year or why one would need a license to marry the person they love or to feed their family or even to collect dead wood to be used as firewood?

Born into Slavery
Who Gives Them This Power Over Us?

As it would seem, however, each individual believes that they were created and born into this world, it's as slaves. Whether it's a forced slavery by our governments or by the various religions that people follow. Here we are, seemingly born free into this world to live, eat, grow, procreate, and prosper for ourselves, our families, and our future.

Unfortunately, this is not the case; we are all slaves…The religions of this world all have a "Master Creator" who demands our loyalty and good behavior for the promise of the most amazing afterlife for all eternity or the opposite for those who choose not to follow their rules of life; they'll spend all eternity in a pit of torture and despair that some call. "Hell". Either way, we are enslaved by their beliefs, customs, and demands of how we are supposed to live our lives under their rule.

The same goes for how we are all enslaved to our government(s), some much worse than others, but let's take the U.S. Government since they are supposed to be governing the "Land of the Free." The people here are supposed to have the ability to live, work, build a business, raise a family, live free, and build a better future without being restricted, controlled, or killed.

The U.S. claims to be ashamed of their slavery days of the past, and yet they are just doing a different version of those days where they actually get not only the labor from the people but they also get to take their wages. Those wages are "Extorted" by the U.S. Government under Force and Fear!

Again, I have to ask…As of 2024, there were at least 340,110,988 people in our population; why the hell are we letting this small amount of thieves to enslave us, control us, kill us, and steal from us?!

So, this question has been asked many times before: "What is the meaning of life?" Were we truly born just be slaves? What is our purpose for existence? From the beginning of time, humans have been enslaving other humans to do their bidding/work. I don't quite know the answer, but slavery seems to be unnatural and definitely not the reason that I am here on this beautiful planet.

Income tax is wrong. You shouldn't be fined for earning a living.

Property tax is wrong. You shouldn't be forced to pay to keep living in a home that you already own.

Sales tax is wrong. You shouldn't be forced to pay someone to allow you to buy something.

Capital gains tax is wrong. You shouldn't be punished for investing in your family's financial future.

Inheritance tax is wrong. Your heirs shouldn't be robbed because you died.

RULES FOR All AMERICAN POLITICIANS

Strict unchangeable laws/rules need to be implemented for any and all American personnel that enter into American politics. Integrity, Honesty, and their unwavering commitment to America.

1. Must be American Born and Raised.
2. Term Limits (2 Terms totaling 4 Years Max) for all positions. Only citizens can vote them back into office.
3. No special treatment, incentives, gas cards, etc.
4. Will only receive a total of $100,000 yearly salary.
5. Will be audited yearly by an independent service that will also be audited yearly for accuracy.
6. Cannot make or pass any laws without citizen votes.
7. Cannot vote themselves raises, protection laws or term limits.
8. Cannot receive Gifts for favors from Corporations, Foreign Nations, or any Special Interest Groups.
9. No longer have free unrestricted access to our Tax Dollars for any use they see fit.
10. Can not use American tax dollars for any foreign nation or national, refugee, asylum seeker, etc.
11. Cannot invest in any trades where they have access to inside information, subject to independent audits.
12. Cannot commit any crime. Instant firing and no returning to any office for offenders.
13. Cannot hide bills inside of bills; all legislation must be transparent.
14. Politicians can not lie or make false promises to their constituents.
15. Cannot pardon people who've committed crimes against the country (Treason).
16. Are not above the law and are subject to being fired and prosecuted for any crime.
17. Have no control over citizens' personal family business or schooling.
18. Can not raise the cost of living for food, fuel, utilities, or insurance.
19. Cannot force additional bills on citizens such as insurance, etc.
20. Cannot raise taxes; everybody pays a 3% base and sales tax, with all tax dollars being used solely for American infrastructure, natural disasters, political salaries, improvements, etc.
21. A government Over-site Committee to keep track of spending, movements, activities, etc.
22. Cannot travel on American Tax Dollars; they must use their own personal funds.
23. Cannot be linked in any way to a foreign government, corporation, or anti-American group of any sort; this would be considered treason.
24. Cannot be bribed or approached by lobbyists for bill persuasions.
25. No traveling back and forth to Washington or to overseas; use Zoom or FaceTime.
26. Single Issue Bills Only - No additives or secret causes.

Things/People that Need to Go
All these Corrupt People / Organizations are Destroying America

* BlackRock Investment Group -
* Vanguard -
* State Street -
* The Rothschilds -
* The Rockefellers -
* Mark Zuckerberg -
* George Soros -
* Nancy Pelosi -
* Chuck Schumer -
* Gavin Newsom -
* IRS - Internal Revenue Service
* Federal Reserve -
* NATO - North Atlantic Treaty Organization
* W.E.F. - World Economic Forum
* D.E.I. - Diversity, Equity and Inclusion
* Woke Ideology -
* NASA - National Aeronautics Space Administration
* CDC - Center for Disease Control
* WHO - World Health Organization
* FDA - Food and Drug Administration
* Shadow Government -
* Deep State -
* Military Industrial Complex -
* Patriot Act -
* U.S.A.I.D. - United States Agency for International Development
* Sanctuary Cities -
* Save the Children Fundraiser -
* Bill and Melinda Gates Foundation -
* Clinton Foundation -
* Cancel Culture -
* FEMA - Federal Emergency Management Agency
* EPA - Environmental Protection Agency

The 'Woke' Generation

If there is anything destroying this Nation and the World, it's this idiotic "WOKE" generation. This movement by top officials, celebrities, and so many weak-minded people has made our country a laughingstock of the world, a complete embarrassment to past generations.

Originally, this fad was about people for Social Injustice, but it has grown to be the downfall of the strength that we once had as a country.

This movement has made the United States so weak and easily accessible to be invaded/overrun by our enemies that it's surprising that they haven't already wiped us out! The only thing stopping China, Russia, North Korea, and Iran from kicking our weak and weird asses is the threat of Nuclear Weapons.

You have China and other countries teaching their children robotics, combat techniques, and many other intellectual advancements while America is teaching our kids that it's okay to be weak, mentally ill, and to be subservient to their corrupt government. The children are our future, and they're watching military men in make-up and dresses, they're watching guys kissing/holding hands on television, an extremely overweight person in charge of our Health Department, men in drag reading books to children in schools, kids don't know which bathroom they should use because this ideology has them questioning their own genetics and gender, kids now believe that men can be pregnant or have periods along with so much more debauchery.

The term **"woke"** originally emerged from African-American Vernacular English (AAVE) and means **being awake to social injustices and inequalities**, particularly those related to race and discrimination. It encompasses an awareness of various social issues, including gender inequality, environmental concerns, and LGBTQ+ rights.

However, the term has evolved and is sometimes used pejoratively to describe individuals or groups perceived as overly politically correct or excessively focused on social justice issues. Overall, being **"woke"** signifies a commitment to recognizing and addressing systemic injustices in society.

The term "woke ideology" has been associated with several negative impacts in America,

Being labeled as "woke" in today's society can have several implications.

1. **Polarization:** Woke ideology can contribute to increased societal polarization, leading to divisions between those who embrace these beliefs and those who oppose them. This can result in heightened tensions and reduced willingness to engage in constructive dialogue.

2. **Censorship and Cancel Culture:** Critics argue that woke ideology can lead to censorship or "cancel culture," where individuals or organizations face backlash for expressing views deemed contrary to progressive values. This may stifle free speech and discourage open discussion.

3. **Identity Politics:** The emphasis on identity can sometimes overshadow broader issues of class and economics, leading to a focus on individual identities rather than collective experiences. This can create friction among different social groups.

4. **Resistance to Nuance:** Woke ideology may sometimes promote a binary view of social issues, where complex situations are oversimplified into right and wrong. This can hinder nuanced discussions and understanding of multifaceted problems.

5. **Backlash and Political Consequences:** The rise of woke ideology has also sparked a backlash, leading to the emergence of counter-movements. This can result in the election of politicians who oppose progressive policies, potentially reversing advancements in social justice.

6. **Corporate Response and Performative Activism:** Some businesses adopt woke principles for marketing purposes rather than genuine commitment, leading to accusations of performative activism. This can dilute the seriousness of social justice issues.

7. **Impact on Education:** Critics argue that an emphasis on woke ideology in educational settings can lead to controversial curriculum changes, creating conflict among parents, educators, and students about the appropriate focus of education.

Cancel culture is a big part of this "woke" ideology and has sparked significant debate and discussions. Its negative effects have included:

1. **Stifling Free Speech:** Individuals may feel hesitant to express their opinions for fear of backlash, leading to a chilling effect on open dialogue and debate for fear of losing their job or being ridiculed by these mentally ill morons.

2. **Fear of Consequences:** People might self-censor or avoid discussing controversial topics, limiting the diversity of viewpoints in public discourse.

3. **Public Shaming:** Cancel culture can lead to intense public shaming, which can have severe emotional and psychological effects on individuals, regardless of their intent or the context of their actions.

4. **Lack of Nuance:** Often, complex issues are oversimplified, leading to black-and-white thinking where individuals are either fully supported or completely condemned without room for understanding or redemption.

5. **Impact on Careers:** Individuals can lose their jobs or face career setbacks due to social media backlash, which can be disproportionate to the offenses they are accused of.

6. **Polarization:** Cancel culture can exacerbate societal divides by creating "us versus them" mentalities, making it harder for different groups to engage constructively.

7. **Misuse of Power:** It can empower individuals to target others for personal grievances, leading to abuse of the cancel culture phenomenon.

8. **Short-lived Impact:** The rapid nature of social media can lead to swift judgments that may not reflect the long-term character or actions of individuals.

Overall, being labeled as "woke" can reflect a commitment to social justice but can also lead to the misguiding and weakening of our people, which in turn destroys our country. This is the movement that has helped bring our country the closest to the movie "Idiocracy."

When I mention how stupid movements ruin the country by dumbing it down, it goes along with the previously mentioned (in books 1 & 2) the **"Ghetto Culture"** *that has turned this country from kids and people working to learn proper English and grammar, dressing well, acting with proper behavior to them not knowing how to talk properly, spell properly, dress with their pants in the proper position (up), or even act like decent human beings.*

It's horrible when all the spelling and grammar online is almost unrecognizable and dumbed down. Even a new "so-called" dictionary has emerged for people who can't speak or spell properly, which is ridiculous. Nobody wants to see the underwear of these people or, worse, the cracks of their asses; nobody wants to take time to decipher what the heck they're saying while speaking to them or trying to read something that they're writing.

Their behavior is atrocious as they feel entitled to a free life without working for it. Unfortunately, their life is at the cost of "Hard Working and Responsible Americans." Because of them and their stealing ways, we can't even go shopping in peace without witnessing a group of them storming a business, grabbing merchandise, and running out with it. We can't shop without everything being locked behind plastic barriers, which is very frustrating, especially when you have employees who are slow and unmotivated to have a job.

What People are Saying

What issues do I have with this:

1. Sexualization of children
2. Underage genital mutilation
3. Underage puberty blocks to trans
4. Schools teaching gender confusion
5. School libraries having porno books
6. Drag shows with children in audience
7. Men competing in women's sports
8. Men in women's locker rooms/bathrooms

- **Jeffrey Sachs** (American Economist): regards the United States as the most Lawless and Dangerous Country in the World today. We are run by a Deep State that operates the largest War Machine in the World.

- **Pete Hegseth:** "Politics should play NO Part in military matters. We are not Republicans, we are not Democrats, we are American Warriors." Our standards will be high, and they will be equal - not equitable. That's a very different word. Equity is all about preferred outcomes and preferred treatment for preferred people and has no place within the Department of Defense."

- **John F. Kennedy** (U.S. President): "There is a plot in the country to enslave every man, woman, and child. Before I leave this high and noble office, I intend to expose this plot."

> **"DEFENDING THE BORDER IS NOT A POLITICAL OPTION. IT IS A CONSTITUTIONAL OBLIGATION,"**

A Failed Government

The forefathers wrote a constitution to be the basis of a free and prosperous country without unwarranted Taxes and especially Government overreaching. A Government to protect the people of this new nation and keep government oversight. However, as is done when any human is in power, that power has gone to their heads, and they have been corrupted and become extremely Tyrannical, believing that they can and do Rule Us.

Their wayward behavior has gotten so out of control that nothing in this country is legitimate; our own government has failed to protect the U.S. Citizens from any and all evils in this world because they themselves have become the largest and worst criminals of them all in this world! The U.S. Government has become Too Big and needs to be dismantled from within and reestablished as "A Government For the People, by The People."

The U.S. Government has become the largest Organized Crime Syndicate in the world, and instead of building and protecting the citizens of this country, they have actually turned against them and become the internal enemy of this nation and its people.

They've (possibly) gone completely against the constitution, changed it to meet their desires, poisoned Americans, killed citizens, destroyed cities and buildings, they've killed presidents and whistleblowers, they extremely overtax their citizens, which starves them, leaves them homeless and without medical care while feeding, housing and providing medical care to foreigners, they start wars for profit and fund foreign wars for profit, sell drugs and run the largest pharmaceutical drug operation in the world, they jail people for committing any and all crimes that they themselves are committing, as they must see them as competition.

The entire system that they've put in place has failed; nothing is for the improvement, betterment, or prosperity of the American people. Everything is about their Globalist Elite Agendas and attempting to force the entire world under their control; they use religions, fear, chemicals, and force to try and reel us all in like blind, stupid sheep. The unfortunate part is that many people are just that and are so weak and gullible that it works.

The legal system is a corrupted money system; the FDA is allowing us to be poisoned by the foods we eat and keeping us sick for the medical/pharmaceutical industries, the DEA runs their own drug operation, the Border Patrol looks the other way and allowed millions of illegal aliens to invade this country. Their medical system isn't about healing and helping, but is instead a massive money-making system. The pharmaceutical industry is all about creating repeat customers and not healing or helping people. Unfortunately, I can go on and on about how we need a Complete Government Reform! They've gotten Too Big, Too Out of Control, Too Powerful, Too Tyrannical, and Way Too Comfortable doing whatever they want and being Unchecked by the People of this country!

A major show of government overreach has been displayed in many ways as the government has now taken control of the lives of OUR children. They've forced their power over the education system, which has completely failed our society by confusing children into not knowing which bathroom to use because these days they are so confused about what gender they are! They've allowed what used to be mentally ill child predators into our schools to read and misinform children. Unfortunately, some of these predators are the teachers themselves who are putting up Gay-Pride flags in their classrooms along with literature for children to read.

Does it make sense that children cannot make any important decisions or choices of their own until 18 or 21, and yet they somehow can now decide what gender they identify as and that they can make a life-altering body-dysmorphic decision without their parents' permission? Children in other countries are learning Robotics, Calculus, Combat Readiness, and multiple High-Tech systems to improve themselves and prepare for the future, while our kids are being raised to not know the difference between a male and female figure, raised into slavery, compliance, confusion, homosexuality, drug addiction, obesity all around weakness and mental illness.

They've allowed and have placed homosexual commercials on television as well as every television show, movie, and cartoon to include homosexual characters and behavior, all suggesting that this is normal. It is NOT normal... All this while the children are NOT learning a damn thing in school that is important. They're being groomed to not only live a mentally ill life of confusion, immorality, and slavery but to fail as decent human beings who are supposed to live in a Free Country.

A wolf pack will follow its prey for many miles until the prey gets too weak to continue running for its life, and then it'll just give up and die at the jaws of the wolves. The government is systematically weakening the citizens of this country and preparing us to be taken over and subservient to whoever will rule this land in years to come. Marijuana and many other drugs will make you dependent, slow you down, and weaken your mind/will; they're confusing the children and making them think that these things are normal. Grooming our children to be weak, confused and easily controlled. They'll be eaten by the wolves if we don't turn things around and save them now!

The government has failed as leaders, representatives, and examples not only to the people of this nation, but to the world. They've shown how a country should NOT be run, and yet they continue to attempt to Force their so-called Democratic ways upon other nations as a better way of life for their citizens. Every system has been corrupted to only see dollar figures and not what's best for the people or society as a whole.

Amazingly, this dysfunctioning government system has attacked and removed other world leaders for doing much less than what they've done for so many decades. Now, it even weaponizes its own Justice System against a Political opponent and, in some cases, against its citizens. Does Dictatorship come to mind? How many Dictators have they over-thrown and taken down for the supposed benefit of the people, and now they are the same or worse because they call themselves by different names?

Trust me; this country has become so weak, disoriented, and embarrassing that if it wasn't for nuclear weapons, we would have been invaded, destroyed, and taken over by many other world power countries such as China, Russia, Iran, North Korea and who knows who else. Those bombs are the only reason we, as a country, still exist. It's just unfortunate that the worst enemy to the people of the United States is now our own government, which could be classified as Domestic Terrorists!

So What's Their End Game

You have to wonder what their plans are for the future. How do they expect to continue on their path of destruction? A country that is run on War and Illness has no future. Do they really think that their current course of action is setting up a strong future for this country? What is their goal? Are they looking to enslave millions of people by killing off the strong in useless wars or by making them all so sick and weak that they'll need their pharmaceutical products?

Their actions don't make sense; these idiots in government have to realize that life is nothing but a moment in time, and no amount of money is going to stop their deaths, nor will they be bringing their riches with them when they go. So what happens once you've driven all of your citizens into absolute poverty or death? Who will pay your taxes and fund your greed?

Do they kill just because they can? Can't they find better ways to limit the world population if that is their goal? How about a positive idea such as asking the world population to halt from procreating for a 2-year term? Not everyone will adhere to the request, but many will and that in itself will drastically bring down or slow down the numbers. My thoughts are that those who are on Welfare and can't/won't take care of themselves shouldn't be having children anyway; they should all be surgically stopped from doing so. Stop the burden on everyone else and the system by preventing unsupported children.

The common term in medicine on day one is said to be "A Patient Cured is a Patient Lost." That does not sound like the oath that doctors and medical professionals take to help people. These days, their main concern is how much money they can make off each individual; that's why they have extraordinarily high prices on every service or product.

Congratulations, idiots, you had a chance to govern the most amazing country in existence and build a strong nation of Free People who work hard and support their families, which could have shown the world how, throughout history, we have learned the proper way to live and run a country. But, your greed and quest for unchecked power have scrambled your brains, and you've blown an amazing opportunity.

Instead, they have shown the world how a country of politicians and not patriots can become so Tyrannical and Corrupt that they will destroy the greatest country in history. They've shown that a country government with no oversight and no limitations can and will turn on their own people and destroy the future of their country for power and financial gain. Clearly, they've shown the world the wrong way to run a country and lit the fuse for America to be another historic failure like so many other powerful nations of the past ie. Persians, Romans, Aztecs, Mongolians, Etc.

All you've done is lost the confidence and trust of your citizens and opened the door to a future takeover by weakening your country. You've attempted to take away our guns, taken away our masculinity, poisoned our food, drugged us all up, destroyed out Patriotism, confused our children and made us a weak nation! The only thing that's stopped countries like Russia, China, North Korea and Iran from joining together and attacking the U.S. is the threat of Nuclear Weapons...Otherwise they'd combine powers and easily come over to whip this queer country's ass!

By Tyson Johnson
July 20, 2016
I have no faith in man as man has no faith in you or me. Man has no desire to be good, man only desires to conquer and destroy. Man is a disease that's spread across the globe, a globe filled with beauty and wonder, a life giving globe covered with food and water for all man, and yet man destroys the globe, burns, and rapes and pillages the globe, man litters upon and pollutes the globe. Man is conceived from affection but grows to hate man, grows to torture and grows to enslave man. Man commits evil against man. Man murders man, man starves man, man rapes man, man abuses
man, man steals from man, man taxes man, man starves man, man controls man, man belittles man, man bullies man, man falsely accuses man, man oppresses man, man judges man, man lies to man, man creates laws for man, man corrupts law, man creates religion, man defiles religion. Man exploits man, man extorts man and man makes living life hard for man.
Man is "The Human Disease"

American Issues / American Solutions
Race Issues

ALLEGED ISSUES: Systemic Racism - Inequality, Unfair Treatment, and Physical Abuse towards the black race by America, its Judicial System, and Law Enforcement. Unfair Treatment and Suppression of the black race by Law Enforcement and other races in America – A separation between the black race and every other race in America.

ARTICLES OF SOLUTIONS:

1. **In order to remove racial issues**, every and all families in America must agree that the current teaching of racial inequality from the past is ineffective and produces a negative effect on the modern-day society where we are attempting to move forward with Racial Equality. Teaching, Dwelling On, and Ingraining the wrongs of the past can only have Negative Mental and Emotional effects on our Children, Progress, and Future of our Country and should be immediately Stopped. Racism Starts in the Home. Each Parent will be responsible for the Positive Teaching and Interaction between races. You and your children will be criminally responsible for any negative actions of racism.

2. **All Law Enforcement will undergo extensive Interracial** Educational Training, Community Social Skills and Improved Use of Force Education to enhance their Public Social Handling. (This training does not mean that if you commit a crime, you will not be dealt with; it means that you will be contacted and dealt with the same amount of respect given to the Law Enforcement Officials on scene – If you choose to be disrespectful and get physical, they can and will get physical enough to affect the arrest). Their Use of Force will be based on your actions!

3. **There shall be 1 Law and Consequence** – A Law for 1, A Law for All – Meaning that if One breaks the law, then the consequences for that crime shall be the Same for All, No Matter their Race, Creed, Color or National Origin. (Simple Rule " –Don't Do the Crime & You Won't Do the Time")

4. **Defunding and Closure of any and all Private Prisons** and additional funding for the number of Prosecutions completed by the District Attorney's Office to reduce the ability to seek a conviction of any kind by any means necessary, which promotes Wrongful Convictions without 100% accuracy.

5. **All Lives Will Matter** - Any and All racial Separation through education, television, radio, and social media shall be outlawed. Only positive racial integration shall be promoted through all the above-named avenues. Racial Hate crimes will have an automatic enhancement added to their sentence. All races have suffered tragedy, whether it was hundreds or thousands of years in the past, and so All races have Grievances against some other race! No one race shall be put above any other, and so All Lives Will Matter, or No Lives Will Matter, regardless of past grievances!

6. **No longer will there be Privileged** or Preferential Treatment in any way towards blacks - The immediate removal of any and all racist organizations, shows, music, educational facilities, promotions, and programs such as BLM, Antifa, NAACP, B.E.T., United Negro College Fund, Black History Month, etc… (Same will go for White Organizations).

7. **You are No longer to refer to yourselves** as "African-Americans" (because that suggests racial separation); you are AMERICANS! The same goes for any and all races living here in America. Be an American, or go back to your Country of Origin!

8. **You ask for Equality and Respect** – So be respectful, Act, Walk, Talk, Dress and Earn the Respect that you Deserve. Show that you are Equal and should be treated as such.

9. **Welfare Programs / Government Assistance** will no longer be a career – Term limits shall be placed on any and all Programs for any and all citizens. One citizen shall no longer be responsible to provide, through taxes or any other means, for another! All able-bodied citizens must work and pay taxes (Note: taxes should be equal for all classes at no more than 5% across the board), and having additional children is no longer a solution for continued or increased aid. If you can't support yourself or your current kids, you shouldn't't have them. We all work, we all pay, and everybody is responsible for caring for themselves and their own family. Equality!

10. **Racial Slurs / Names** - No longer shale racial slurs be used to describe any race or person, such as Nigger, Whitey, Coon, Cracker, Spear Chucker, White Boy, Chink, Zipper Head, Spick, Gook, Wap, etc…

<u>The Proof is Clear and Present</u>

There is an overwhelming amount of evidence of the treachery, corruption, fraud, lies, treason, murder, theft, and so much more that has been perpetrated by the U.S. Government that it is clear that they can not be trusted with our money, health, food, safety, security, children, country or our future. Any and all power needs to be removed from these people, as they clearly cannot handle the responsibilities of running a country or the lives of its citizens that occupy it.

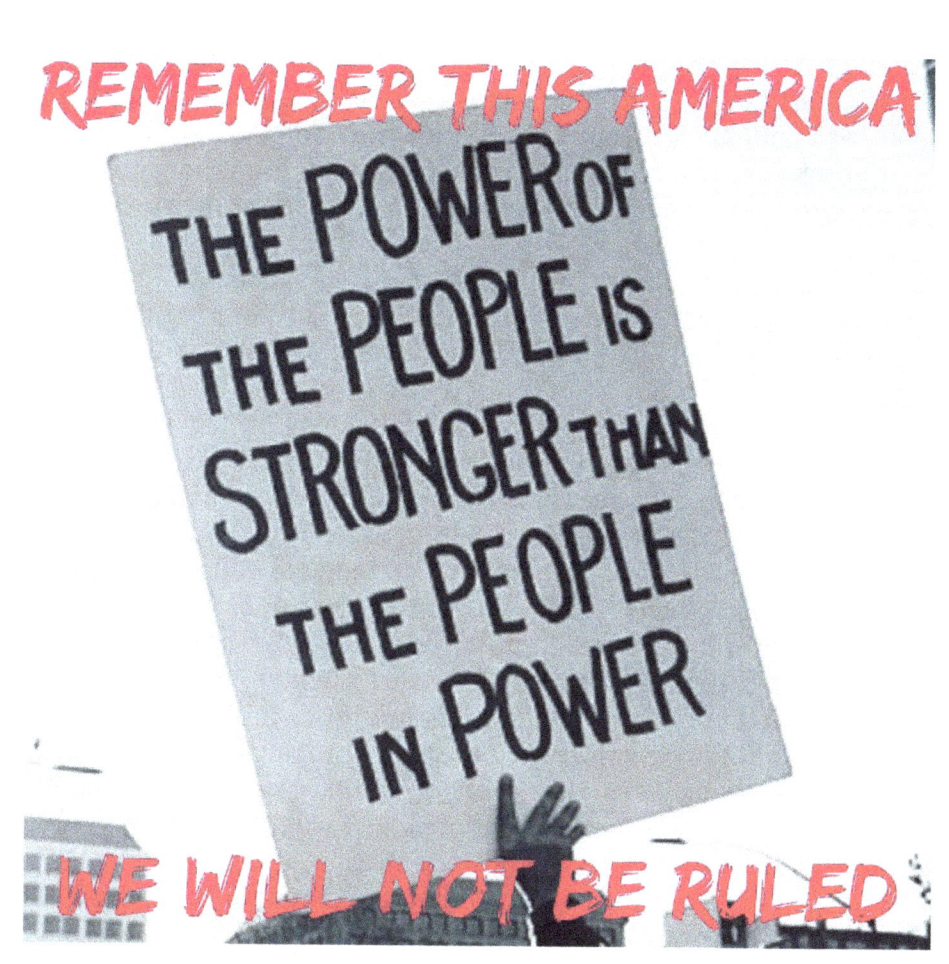

In Closing

Unfortunately, the United States Government has proven for decades that they cannot handle the responsibility of running this country, having control, or making/enforcing the laws. They're worse than bad children who constantly break the house rules, attempt to hide their crimes, and cry foul when they get caught. Even more unfortunately, we citizens are like weak parents who enable the bad behavior of the children as we continue to allow such actions and even continue to fund the troublemakers. If we stop funding and enabling their bad behavior, they won't be able to continue.

So, as you can see, the greatest issue in this great Nation is unfortunately, its own Government. How much more proof do we need to see that these people and their corrupt systems all need to go? They haven't learned a damn thing from past empires that no longer exist because of their own internal corruption, greed, lies, and murder. Those who have been voted for and entrusted to help lead, guide, and protect our nation, our people, and our future have become so Tyrannical and Corrupt with what seems to be unchecked and unchallenged Power. They are evil and have agendas that will surely destroy this country and the world as we know it.

History has been forgotten, and the once great empires are gone for the same exact reason that's going on today. They may feel like they're going to live forever and they'll be rulers of billions of people, but just as the Romans, Egyptians, Persians, Philistines, Aztecs, and so many more empires found out...You only have a limited time of destroying your people and your country before everything that you are and have tried to do comes crumbling down, and you're reduced to no or little existence!

This country started as a lie (Columbus discovering this land, a partnership with the Native People who actually did already live here, the hiding of the "Genocide" and enslavement against the Native People of this land, the

It's Sad and Unfortunate that the Government of this Country hates its own people so much that they do everything evil that they can to destroy them such as Starvation, Homelessness, Propaganda, Scare Tactics, Mind Control, Misdirection, Distractions, Poisoning our Food, Infecting people with Viruses, Over Taxation, Taxing them in to Poverty, Burning their Homes down as was done in Hawaii and now currently in Los Angeles (Pacific Palisades), Forcing Poisonous Vaccines on them, they Lie to us, Cheat us and Steal from us, they Ignore the U.S. Constitution and the Laws of this land for their own benefit, they Create Laws for the people and set themselves above them, they Create Wars both Foreign and Domestic, they Ignore the Needs of their own people while Catering to foreign needs, they ruthlessly enforce laws against the people that they themselves break on a daily basis such as pedophilia, Drug Trafficking, Extortion, Corruption, Genocide, Murder, Cover-Ups, Sex Trafficking, Human Trafficking, Slavery, Insurance Scamming, Creating more laws to Restrict and Enslave the people of this country. They Destroy their Own Buildings, Kill their own Citizens, Shoot down their own Planes.

They Cover Up their Own Crimes with More Crimes, they allow the Flooding of their country with Foreign Invaders, Attempt to play World Police and push their Globalist Agendas on others by Force or Fear, They attempt to Restrict our Freedoms, or Privacy, our Security, Use Social Media and Technology against us, Hide the Truth and Censor us, Drive wedges against different races and turn the people against each other, they Discriminate, Illegal use of our Tax Dollars (Misappropriation of Funds), they've created Devastating Disasters such as Extreme Weather Conditions and Fires to Destroy people's lives, LA Mayor cut fire fighter funding by 17.6 million dollars months before the fires to help Homelessness, Almost Nothing was done for the homeless and millions of dollars are unaccounted for, the government over-reach has gotten so out of control where they are now making decisions on how you can or should raise your children, they're destroying this country with their "Woke" agenda which has put transgenders in front of children in schools, allowed boys and grown men in girls bathrooms, allowed men in to women's sports, they've allowed people to "Identify" as something different and pretend to be that (which would be ok as people should be able to pretend to be whatever they want, just as long as they don't expect the rest of the world to have to go along with their illusions).

They've allowed criminals out of jail and allowed retailers who are trying to make a living be vandalized and robbed by criminals with little to no repercussions. They allow mentally ill same-sex couples to adopt children, which obviously confuses a child, and in some cases, they are exposed to and or abused by those people; they illegally track, surveil and listen in on the citizens of this country, they kill any Whistleblowers that expose their illegal activities (as they'll probably do to me...lol), recently, the Speaker of the House, Mike Johnson, just passed legislation that gives the IDF (Israeli Defense Force) U.S. Health Benefits! Can you believe that bullshit? These corrupt ass backward politicians feed, house, and provide "FREE" healthcare to Foreigners while American Citizens are Starving, Homeless, and can hardly, if at all, afford Health Care!

Sadly and Unfortunately, The United States Government is the largest Organized Crime Network in the World. They are unfit to run this country and need to be removed immediately.

Everything, or at least most of everything that we grew up learning, has been a lie, a scam, a misdirection, or a distraction. These Mentally corrupt idiots can't just let people live and prosper in life, grow families, and enjoy this beautiful planet without trying to control and enslave us. They all need to be hunted down, captured, prosecuted, and destroyed so that a new set of organized systems can be set in place that'll ensure the growth of prosperity and the future of this country.

Some American Issues that need Correction

* Let's restore the U.S. Constitution
* Set Terms for all Government Officials
* No electronic or mail in voting
* No more Income Tax
* 10% Federal Tax across the board
* No more Foreign Aid
* Closed Borders
* All Tax Dollars go to U.S.
* U.S. Veterans to be supported
* No American Citizens in the streets
* No selling U.S. land to foreign investors

* Relaxed gun laws for U.S. Citizens
* Scientific clarity between Male & Female
* Remove the over-reach and power of the IRS
* Clean up, rebuild and restore American cities
* No Government involvement in family affairs
* Restore family and American values.
* No exploitation or marketing sexuality to children
* Removal or lowering of many licenses and fees
* Restore a business's right to defend their assets
* Cost of living and all retail prices to be rolled back
* Prosecution of all Epstein Island perpetrators
* Prosecution of Corrupt Government Officials
* Investigation in to all political funds and accounts
* Reduction of Government Overreach
* Reduction of Government Spending
* Revision of Legal System
* Revision of Welfare Systems
* Revision of the U.S. School System

For The People, By The People!

No Politician / No Actor - Just an American

Some Reasons that I don't trust the Government

* Native Americans / Indigenous People
* 9/11
* Building #7
* JFK
* Covid 19 Pandemic
* H1N1 - SARS - Bird Flu - Monkey Pox
* MK Ultra
* Operation Northwoods
* Operation Paperclip
* Operation Fast and Furious
* Waco
* Ruby Ridge
* Operation Mockingbird
* Tuskegee Experiments
* NSA Spying on us
* Gulf of Tonkin
* Flint Water Crisis
* Chicago Black Sites
* Iran Contra
* Gary Webb
* Edward Snowden
* NDAA
* Patriot Act
* Bilderberg Group
* Abu Granhib
* Bohemian Grove
* Guantanamo Bay
* Benghazi
* WW2
* 2020 elections and administration from 2020 - 2024
* And So Much More...

__Final Words From The Author__

The Keys to Restoration are to Investigate, Locate, Apprehend, Expose, and Prosecute every single one of them. The people of this nation need to see repercussions for the unlawful actions of all these corrupt, law-breaking, and tyrannical politicians, elites, and celebrities. Restore the faith in the legal system and prove that...

"NOBODY is above the LAW"!

Show the people that everybody is accountable for their actions no matter their position(s) in this country; you can and will be prosecuted for your crimes. The people are sick of seeing all the evidence and exposed crimes without seeing anyone going to prison, just as we would for much lesser offenses.

For the crimes of Tyranny, Corruption, Extortion, Fraud, and Treason against the People, States, and Country...

The People of the United States want Justice!

About the Author

Tyson Johnson–A New England Native with the blood of American Patriots running through his veins, Tyson now resides and works in Southern California, where he owns and operates his hand-built business. As a natural-born fighter, Tyson is encouraged to stand up for what he believes in, which is the values he grew up learning and living in America: **"There are consequences for your actions, both good and bad."** With the drastic downslide of American culture, finding out that most of what he's learned growing up was all lies, and with a deteriorating way of life, Tyson is concerned for the future of the children that he instructs, the citizens of his country and the future of this once great nation. The United States has been on the fast track to destruction by the very people who had been elected and entrusted to serve and protect it. Their time must come to an end, and America must be restored to its people and values.

www.ingramcontent.com/pod-product-compliance
Lightning Source LLC
Chambersburg PA
CBHW080519030426
42337CB00023B/4572